AVOIDING MARTYRDOM: THE CATHOLIC CHURCH IN THE UNITED STATES

FREDERICK J. SNEESBY

WESTBOW
PRESS
A DIVISION OF THOMAS NELSON
& ZONDERVAN

Cover Photo: Lily Sneesby

Excerpt from Evangelii Nuntiandi by Pope Paul VI. Copyright © 2014 by Libreria Editrice Vaticana. Reprinted by permission of Libreria Editrice Vaticana.

Excerpt from NIGHT by Elie Wiesel, translated by Marion Wiesel. Translation copyright © 2006 by Marion Wiesel. Reprinted by permission of Hill and Wang, a division of Farrar, Straus and Giroux, LLC

"Rich Woman, Poor Woman" appeared in the July 1985 issue of Sojourners magazine (www.sojo.net) and is excerpted here with permission.

ME AND BOBBY MCGEE
Written by Fred L. Foster & Kris Kristofferson
© 1969 Combine Music Corp. All rights administered by Sony/ATV Music Publishing LLC., 424 Church Street, Nashville, TN 37219. All rights reserved. Used by permission.

WestBow Press books may be ordered through booksellers or by contacting:

WestBow Press
A Division of Thomas Nelson & Zondervan
1663 Liberty Drive
Bloomington, IN 47403
www.westbowpress.com
1 (866) 928-1240

ISBN: 978-1-4908-6335-1 (sc)
ISBN: 978-1-4908-6336-8 (hc)
ISBN: 978-1-4908-6334-4 (e)

Library of Congress Control Number: 2014959042

Printed in the United States of America.

WestBow Press rev. date: 2/3/2015

CONTENTS

ACKNOWLEDGEMENTS

I do not have the memory or the level of self-awareness to be able to recognize everyone and everything that contributed to the creation of this book. Parents, brothers and sisters, extended family, childhood experiences, schoolmates, friends, teachers, travels, education and work, struggles and satisfactions, co-workers in the Church, parishioners, colleagues, my family, are all somehow brought forward to each new day and new effort. With God's grace we receive and offer what is good and try to identify and extend what is of value. This book is no different. In the process of receiving, adding to, and passing on, it is always wise to acknowledge that much of what we do pass on does not originate in us. And so I write this book ever mindful of and grateful for what I have been given.

I particularly want to acknowledge Kathleen Beauchene for reading through the text with an editor's eye and offering corrections and suggestions that always improved the writing. Sr. Marian Steffens O.C.D. was kind enough to read the manuscript and offer very sound advice. I also looked for counsel to my good friend Fr. Richard Weisenberger who has taught me much by word and example over the years, and who is an inspiring servant of God and His People. Fr. Kevin Codd's beautiful writing on pilgrimage was an invaluable reference. My friend and classmate Michael Tremmel was so generous in sharing his experience in Zimbabwe. I am grateful to them and I add the necessary disclaimer that they cannot be blamed for the shortcomings of the book.

My wife Sandra and our daughters Grace and Lily deserve special recognition and thanks. Besides the practical contributions of allowing me to bounce ideas off them and to carve out time for writing, they are a tabernacle for me. Most relevant to the themes of this book, it is through loving them and being loved by them that I am able to say that, yes, there are people for whom I would give my life.

INTRODUCTION

I t was an embarrassing letter to receive. I hadn't heard from him in three years, but we went back many years: back to college seminary days, back to years in Belgium when our rooms were across the hall from each other and we studied Theology, discussed the latest interpretations of the Resurrection and enjoyed many a Belgian beer together.

We both returned to our home state to begin careers in the priesthood – fresh troops for an old battle – and started out in healthy, suburban parishes. There wasn't much contact after that; the demands of so many parishioners and the desire to make an impact left little room for discussions of theology over a glass of beer. And then, he left. He left the priesthood. I didn't know exactly why although I had heard of disagreement with the bishop over assignments. I reacted to his resignation the way I reacted to the departures of several other priests - "good" priests. I considered it a personal matter. "Only he knows the reasons for his leaving," I would think. I tried to respect that, to give credit to their freedom and personal responsibility. But in my mind I added on other factors, idle speculations about the genesis of such a life-changing decision. Those "other factors" almost always came under the heading of "personal weakness": a flaw in their preparation, an unresolved conflict or doubt in the development of their vocation, a misunderstanding about the nature or mission of the priesthood, unrealistic expectations of ministerial success, the inability to maintain a strong celibate commitment, personal frustration over the slow change in the post-Vatican II church. Alongside my respect for this "very personal decision," I felt anger. "It really hurts the mission," I remember saying to a co-worker in the parish. "That's one less talented person whom we needed for the task at hand," I would say. As one "good priest" left, and then another, and then another, there was a growing sense of abandonment and a quiet resentment as I worked overtime for God's people.

There wasn't much time or energy for brooding over these departures. There was the initial surprise, some days of digesting the news, a few conversations about it with other priests and church workers, and then we moved on. The ex-priest was now part of the living dead - he was now part of another world and any contact would be strained and artificial. I never called. I never wrote.

So, I was surprised to receive his letter – and ashamed. It wasn't an angry letter. It wasn't accusatory. It wasn't negative or critical in any way. In fact, the letter from the ex-priest was supportive and encouraging, which only made me more uncomfortable because now I was an ex-priest. After ten years, I had left the priesthood, and I was receiving from him something I had not given to him or others who left the priesthood – support and understanding.

I learned that I had been callous. The only remedy for that is to ask forgiveness and to walk a different path. But I learned more. Very soon after my own resignation, I began to realize that leaving the priesthood was not only a "personal matter." I knew that there was more to my leaving than any flaws in my preparation, conflicts or doubts surrounding my vocation, misunderstandings of the priesthood, unrealistic expectations about the outcome of my work, an inability to remain celibate, or any personal frustration about changes in the Catholic Church. It was more than a personal matter although, without question, my leaving the priesthood had been very "personal," shaking the core of my identity. It was rooted in my strengths and weaknesses, my history and my goals, my search for spiritual maturity, and in recent changes and discoveries in my life.

But there was more at work. There was, amid all the struggles that just had to do with me, a disquiet about the Church, an unsettling sense that the Church was off-track, off-center. I had worked all those years confident that the goals of the Church were worthy of all my energies and now, as the Church kept moving in a certain direction, I had stopped walking with it and decided to go another way. Along with the knowledge that there were some things wrong with me was the realization that there were some things wrong with the Church. My personal search for what God wanted me to do had crossed the path of a wider investigation into what God needed the Catholic Church to do. Personal flowed into universal. As I began to fill in answers about myself, I found insights and issues that touched upon the life of the whole Church.

It also dawned on me that many other Catholics had probably had similar journeys and that my "personal issues" intersected with those of many, many believers: women, the divorced, homosexuals, minorities or others who "jumped ship" to join other denominations. I had failed to see when others left that perhaps what I understood as individual struggles were really commentaries on the state of the Church. As a priest, I had conveniently boxed their pain and struggle into the narrow confines of "personal matters" and simply did not, or would not, recognize how all these individual stories were really about me and my congregation and my diocese and my Church and about all who seek the religious life. The failure to observe and admit this connection was, on my part, a purely defensive reaction by someone who was part of the established order, someone whose best interests were served by remaining undisturbed. It is embarrassing to admit that I only saw the connection when it was "happening to me." Perhaps it could only be so.

As an ex-priest standing outside of the Church, I saw many more of what I deemed to be its shortcomings and I experienced the impulse to sound the alarm, to shake the faithful from complacency, insisting, "Don't you see that we're drifting further and further away from our real purpose? Don't you realize that all those things we hold most dear in our religion, all the rituals and customs, all the structures and traditions, all that gives us a sense of being "Catholic" and graced, are slowly being emptied of meaning? Don't you understand that if we just keep attending Mass every week, following our religious life as we always have, and continuing on the present course of the Catholic Church that we will end in the wrong place?" But my impulse was deadened by the knowledge that people will not act upon the ills of the Church or even bother to look at them unless they are personally affected by them, just like me. And so I took a deep breath and prepared for the long haul of reform and change. Sudden conversion, like St. Paul's, is very rare. Mostly, it takes place inch by inch. We are dragged along by God's grace reluctant and, sometimes, not even knowing why or where we're going. It is that way for individuals and even more so for large groups and institutions like the Catholic Church. The realist will say that things will never change; the optimist hopes for excruciatingly slow change.

As Jesus pointed out, reform begins in our own hearts. Complaining about the Church, pointing out its faults, crying for change, is all empty talk unless it is preceded and accompanied by "taking the beam from one's own eye." Every pointed remark, every critical insight, is reflected on me. Am I living up to the ideals of which I speak? The urgency I felt to cry, "Reform!" was slowed by the knowledge that I had hardly searched out the scope and depth of what life in Christ has to offer, that I had only slightly responded to the challenge of the Gospel. Then and now, my hopes for the Church are coupled with my own struggle because the realization of Jesus' dream for the Church and the World is dependent, if even in the smallest way, on the depth of my response to him.

I began then, twenty-five years ago at this writing, to live a different vocation - of husband and, eventually, father. It has been my chance, given to me by God, to learn how to love. I do know more than I did back in my rectory days but I also am more aware of what I do not know and I have been humbled by the immense task of love and am more awed than ever when I see this task projected onto the universe God created. With glimpses of what God intended for this creation and knowing how far away it is from being that, I am more certain than ever that the Church is to play a crucial role in its reclamation. That being said, I have no new revelation, no sure dogma that holds the key to how the Church will fulfill its mission. I have questions and notions, suggestions and hopes that I will write down in this book and share. Perhaps this writing will be taken up into a larger dialogue and course of action that will be constructive and positive even if it contains disagreement and painful realizations.

Many years have passed since I left the priesthood. Building a marriage and a family and being consumed by the struggles of everyday life have not extinguished my attachment to the Church nor my idealism about its place in the world. I still expect that the Church should be an instrument of salvation even though I have witnessed so many more reasons to be cynical, to lower my expectations, and to be content with the mediocrity that is endemic in our institutions and characteristic of much of our lives. I still find myself disappointed that the Church is not living up to its calling even as I recognize my own falling short of glory. My story continues to be part of the larger tale of the Church even though I stand at its margins and am daily more persuaded of the impossibility of its mission. I remain nagged by the admonition to "run so as to win" as individuals and as a Church. We can do much better.

This book is an examination of that "better" territory, a look at where the Catholic Church in the United States stands and where it might go. It presumes there is a crucial intersection of the personal and the universal, not only in understanding the issues of the Church and World that affect us all, but also in acting to bring about change and progress. If each person will pause to see and think about his position in the Church, he can take responsibility for it and use it to bring about fundamental reform for the sake of the Gospel. If each person can take her religious life off "automatic pilot" and question the value of what she does religiously Sunday after Sunday, week after week, then she could break out of her spiritual routine and begin with others to move toward what Jesus had in mind when he walked the earth.

This overlay of the personal and the universal springs from the same spirit as Matthew 25: 31-46 in which Jesus insists that the experience of the many, even of the many "least," is also his experience. Paul also cannot shake this belief that we are inexorably attached: "If one member suffers, all the members suffer with it; if one member is honored, all the members share its joy" in the one body which is Christ and all those who belong to Him. This spirit is so foreign to our present-day experience of isolation in an increasingly fragmented world. Although we are aware of much that happens in the world, we are also detached from it as spectators, and we are powerless to touch all that is "out there" or to affect it in any way. While we witness what is happening in the world, we are passive in the face of it all and are barely able to work ourselves up to be interested or concerned. Our own survival and that of our families occupies us so much that it is very hard to break out of our isolation to go beyond ourselves to make any meaningful contact with the "neighbor" near or far.

The hope that people will combine the personal and the universal, that they will be compelled to action because they come to see their own destinies entwined with that of the Church, rests on another assumption, that religion matters. Perhaps a majority of people think that religion is irrelevant and, at best, "window dressing" in the day-to-day business of life. That may even be the state of religion as it is sometimes practiced, but I think that Jesus intended religion to make a difference; he intended that religion be the means through which the world would be saved and made whole again. The book doesn't make any sense unless this desire is assumed; otherwise, who really cares what happens in or to the Catholic Church, or any church? Why get excited about what is preached or practiced by the Church if nothing is really at stake? If religion were just a nice extra in life, then the problems of the Church and any issues raised in this book would just be of passing interest but have no real bearing on what really matters in this world. But if you share this belief that the Church can or should be an instrument of salvation for the world, then read on.

CHAPTER ONE

FIFTH GRADE MARTYRS IN A FAR-AWAY CHURCH

We were ready to be killed for our Catholic faith. At least I was. I just assumed everyone else was too although I never asked them. I just assumed that any fifth grader worth his salt was willing to do whatever it took to defend the faith against the Communists. To others, eleven years old may seem young to contemplate martyrdom, but we in the fifth grade at St. Edward School had read many a biography of young saints: eleven, twelve and thirteen year olds who were called upon to give the ultimate testimony. Our age did not disqualify us. After all, we were spending this year preparing for Confirmation, one of the seven Catholic sacraments by which we would become "soldiers of Christ." No one thought that too much was being expected of these kids. No. The religious sisters, the parish priests and our parents were deadly serious about our training for Christ's army: warriors in the fight for God's kingdom against evil.

This training was two-pronged. First, there was memorization to be done. Seventy-seven questions and answers were printed on mimeo (there were no copy machines in those days, thanks be to God because we probably would've been assigned more questions) and distributed. We had to know them cold and we would be quizzed on them by one of the parish priests. I spent many evenings in the parlor with my parents going over and over the questions, questions about the nature of Confirmation, the gifts and fruits of the Holy Ghost (he or she was not yet known as the Holy Spirit), the ritual and symbols of the sacrament, and what we would be equipped to do by receiving this sacrament.

The second part of the training was motivational. There were stories. Heroes and heroines. From the apostles, transformed by the Holy Ghost at the "first Confirmation" from cowards into witnesses who preached in the face of ridicule, torture and death, to St. Tarcisius who gave his life protecting the Eucharist, to the Crusaders who gave their all to fight against the unbelievers (this was before the age of ecumenism), to St. Maria Goretti who was brave enough to choose virtue instead of a life of sin, all the way to Bishop Walsh who was imprisoned and tortured by the Chinese Communists in our own lifetime. The stakes were high: their individual efforts had eternal significance. The success or failure of Christ's mission depended on their courage. We were joining ranks with them by Confirmation, becoming Soldiers of Christ.

I'm sure this rite of passage meant something in every day and age. But for us in 1962, being confirmed was especially impressive. We were in the teeth of the Cold War. The Communists had crushed freedom in Hungary, they beat us to outer space with Sputnik, our spies were shot down and on trial in Moscow, their leader was yelling in the United Nations that he would "bury" us, they were 90 miles away from our shores in Cuba, they had huge armies to accompany a doctrine of world domination, they were godless, and they had the atomic bomb.

We expected them to appear at our school at any minute.

I am not exaggerating. In our grammar school years, air raids were commonplace. We would run in from playing in the street and lie down on the floor to practice for an atomic attack. We would rehearse crouching under our desks at school in case the attack came during school hours. Again and again, probable scenarios were described to us in which the Communists would come into our school with their weapons drawn. The nuns would, of course, be shot immediately. We would be rounded up, taken from our parents, and brought to camps to be brainwashed in Communist doctrine.

Our immediate goal was to elude the enemy and make our way over to the church where we were to go to the tabernacle and consume the Blessed Sacrament before the Communists could desecrate it. Beyond that, we were to resist any ideological bullying by the Reds and boldly announce our faith and our intention to keep that faith even if it meant our deaths, which we knew it would.

The weak, and we suspected there were weak fifth-graders (probably the ones who did not know all seventy-seven answers), would give in to the first hint of torture and renounce the faith, saying right away that they were not Catholics.

The Communists never came. We were confirmed, promoted to the sixth grade, the clock of history struck 1963, and the maelstrom of cultural change that was the 1960's began to swirl uncontrollably. By 1973, our society and our Church would be completely different. The world of 1973 was radically altered from the world of 1963. It was not just a matter of fast-paced technological changes as we are experiencing today that, in turn, affect the culture. Fundamental change occurred. Generations no longer related to each other in the same way. Gender roles and relationships were fundamentally questioned. The status of governments and institutions was reduced. Authority in general didn't, well, hold any authority. Truth and beauty and goodness became relative terms. Family structures were re-defined. A decade begun in idealism and optimism ended in materialism and cynicism.

Almost six decades later, the memories of that era's Catholic Church in America seem very far away indeed, as does the society as a whole of the 1950's and '60's. The reality of the time is well-revised in the remembering and there are tendencies to be nostalgic or to look back with some wistfulness. The fact is that they really were not the greatest of times. The rigidity of class and race and gender seem unbearable to twenty-first century eyes. The discrepancies between the values people proclaimed and the ones they actually lived reveal a fragility about the prevailing culture that makes the chaos and breakdown of the ensuing years understandable.

Ought we go back to that time? No, we shouldn't and we can't. The virtues of that time period are far outweighed by the defects. But virtues there were. If we were to reach back into that era of the Church marked by insular thinking, we would find some things of value, traits of the Church that were lost during the closing years of the 20th century.

My comrades and I, the fifth-grade confirmees, were engaged in the struggle of good against evil. How welcome would it be for us living in the beginning of the twenty-first century to have moral, political, spiritual, and economic battle lines so clearly and neatly drawn! In the present time, we trip over the definitions of "good" and "evil." It is hard to find agreement on what is of value, and labeling anything as "evil" is pretty much left up to the individual. It is very rare, except for the occasional epic movie like the "Star Wars" series or the more recent "Narnia" films, that we can identify the "good guys" and the "bad guys."

This murkiness about what is right and what is wrong may have started to be stirred up in the Korean War when, in contrast to the Second World War, the purpose of expending the lives of so many was unclear, an uncertainty that was taken up anew further south and further down the timeline in Vietnam. It wasn't that the war in Southeast Asia wrought any more destruction than WW II; it was just that we couldn't seem to justify it.

What are the moral struggles in which average Catholics are engaged today? Very few can be named. None of them approaches the sweep and seriousness of the battle we waged in the fifth grade against a worldwide godless organization. Those sorts of struggles presume that there are enemies, an "Us" and a "Them." They require battle lines, some demarcation of what is to be lost and what gained. They make no sense unless there is a lot at stake, matters worth dying for, causes that can be championed. We had all of that back in the early '60's when even the choices and actions of an eleven-year-old mattered and martyrdom was a possible outcome for even the average Catholic.

Not everyone is called to be a martyr. It is a particular vocation, a calling, a special role that a person plays in the spiritual life of the Church that blends in to the other believers' functions, as St. Paul explains in I Corinthians 12 7ff,

> To each person the manifestation of the Spirit is given for the common good. To one, the Spirit gives wisdom in discourse, to another the power to express knowledge. .... The body is one and has many members, but all the members, many though they are, are one body and so it is with Christ .... You, then, are the body of Christ ... God has set up in the church first apostles, second, prophets, third teachers, then miracle workers, healers, assistants ...,

Jesus is alive in the world through a community, not just individuals. It is in the gathering and sharing of everyone's gifts in the Church that a complete and mature spiritual life can be experienced. Not everyone is a teacher but we need teachers in the Church to be complete. Not everyone devotes his life to prayer but we need pray-ers in the Church to be whole. Not everyone is called to serve the poor but there must be these servants in the Church if the fullness of Jesus is to be shown. Not everyone is called to be a martyr but martyrdom must be a part of the Church's life for it to be complete.

What exactly is the role of martyrdom in the Church? It was Tertullian, a great and controversial writer in the early Church, who wrote that "the blood of the martyrs is the seed of the Church." In other words, the growth of the faith springs from martyrdom. How, exactly, does that work?

Martyrdom is a measure of a person's commitment to the faith. Can a deeper commitment be imagined? The martyr stakes everything on what he or she believes or, more precisely, on the person in whom he or she believes, Jesus. The martyr is willing to make the ultimate sacrifice and to say by doing so that being a follower of Jesus is of greater value than even life itself. Anyone who would hear this message would conclude that this "life in Christ" that the martyr has found must be very valuable indeed, the "pearl of great price" that the merchant in Jesus' story finds and then sells everything he has to buy (Matthew 13: 44-46). When a person finds something so significant and meaningful as to be willing to sacrifice his or her life for it, that is very attractive and compelling to other people.

Martyrdom is a measure of the comprehensiveness of a person's life orientation. The faith is not just one among other considerations in his or her life, it is the principal concern, the central factor in a person's makeup that integrates every other aspect of that person's life and which directs every choice and action by that person.

Martyrdom not only signals the depth and breadth of a person's commitment, but it indicates the degree to which "life in Christ" is in opposition to the dominant culture. If Church membership and all it entails did not threaten or call into question the prevailing culture, why would it elicit such a violent reaction? Who would respond to the presence of a believer with such drastic action unless this person's devotion radically challenged the perpetrator's values and priorities and goals?

Martyrdom, then, gauges the willingness of the Church to fulfill its mission of bringing the world to share the life of Jesus. It measures the degree to which the Church focuses its resources and energies on preaching the message of Jesus, witnessing to his presence through the everyday lives of believers and communities, and transforming the world into what God intended it to be. Martyrdom demonstrates that believers place the highest value on sharing Jesus' life and will fulfill the mission of drawing others into that life without counting the cost.

If there are no martyrs or no one willing to be a martyr, the Church cannot be the Church; it cannot realize its purpose. Martyrdom is an essential element in the life of the Church. Not everyone is called to be a martyr, but everyone must be prepared to suffer martyrdom. Openness to martyrdom is an essential component of a healthy Church.

As odd as it may sound in the beginning of the twenty-first century in the United States, martyrdom was a considered option for American Catholics in the late 1950's and early 1960's. How can it be that martyrdom was imaginable in the United States not that long ago and today being killed for what you believe would be very hard to accomplish?

For starters, although Catholics had been present from the earliest days of the United States, Roman Catholicism was still a foreign religion in the 1950's or, better stated, was a religion of foreigners. Many Catholics were first and second generation immigrants from Catholic countries and still very conscious of being "Irish" or "Italian" or "Polish." When a person was asked what nationality he was, the first answer was not "American," it was "French" or "German" or whatever place was the ancestors' country of origin. National identity was preserved in foods and language and shared history and customs and neighborhood and in the associations forged by newcomers to America to ensure survival. Being Catholic was deeply imbedded in this consciousness, breeding not only an awareness by the Catholic immigrant of being distinctive but a corresponding sense of "otherness" on the part of established Americans, a realization that they were dealing with people who were different.

In the Church I grew up in, Catholics married Catholics, Catholics babies were baptized ASAP and they were named after saints. They went to Catholic schools, they played in Catholic sports leagues, they associated in Catholic men's and women's and youth groups, their social lives were circumscribed by church-sponsored ham & bean suppers, penny socials, Communion breakfasts, parish picnics and outings. Feastdays marked the calendar and many, whose origins lay in hometowns back in the old country, were days-long celebrations that dominated neighborhoods and cities and that featured processions and carnivals and public expressions of devotion. Catholics networked in the Knights of Columbus and the Rosary Sodality; they did good works through the St. Vincent de Paul Society and gathered with other Catholic families in the Christian Family Movement. When they were sick, they went to Catholic hospitals and when they died, they were buried in Catholic cemeteries. When I was a kid, we were forbidden to join the YMCA or to enter a non-Catholic church building; the public school was referred to as the "Protestant school."

Catholics did not eat meat on Fridays. They fasted often and observed special obligations that seemed stricter than other religious denominations. Attendance at weekly Mass was both mandated and presumed. They decorated their homes and yards with images of saints and Jesus and his Mother, Mary. Once a year, they left church with ashes on their heads or carrying palms. Their services were conducted in Latin and they had powerful prayer customs like the Rosary and Novenas and Benediction and Adoration.

The Catholic Church was its own world, easily recognizable by those within and outside its boundaries. I remember that I did not feel any compunction to "blend into" or to compromise with the surrounding culture. The Church was sufficient.

Back in the mid-1800's, the nativists were terrified of the growing waves of Catholic immigrants. They fought against and targeted Catholics, restricted their economic and political activity, and nurtured anti-Catholic sentiment and action, the strains of which remain to this day. They feared that Catholics could never be true Americans, that their allegiance would be to the Pope and not the

President, that they would adhere to Catechism before Constitution, and that they would, thus, undermine the United States. In the capital city of my home state, the Know-Nothings (as one of the nineteenth century nativist movements was called) marched on the local Catholic high school with torches to burn it down only to be turned back by an equally-armed mob of Catholics who had ringed the school on Broad Street.

If they had stepped into my grammar school classrooms in the mid-twentieth century, their fears about Catholics would not have been allayed. In the Cold War, our impulse was to defend the faith, not necessarily the country. In our estimation, the most strategic target was the tabernacle not the city hall; all that mattered was the battlefield of the spirit. The Know-Nothings would have seen the distinct identity of mid-1900's Catholicism and shuddered at the discontinuities between what was Catholic and what was American.

For Catholics, however, there was no conflict between the two. Just when American Catholicism was riding high institutionally before the crash of the mid-1960's, the melding of Catholicism and Americanism was crystallized in the candidacy and election of John F. Kennedy, the first Catholic U.S. President. In him, the Catholic immigrant had finally "made it," achieving a legitimacy and acceptance in American society that Catholics had not enjoyed. We were so American that we could be elected President.

Religion was an issue in that election, so much so that John Kennedy addressed it in a major speech to the Greater Houston Ministerial Association in September 1960. As a Catholic, I cringe when I read that speech today. If I had known about or read the speech when I was nine years old while anticipating that my parents would be voting for Kennedy while Johnny's Protestant parents down the street would not be, I would have been completely confused if not scandalized.

Then Senator Kennedy said some important things about the right of Catholics to participate fully in the life of the nation, the duty of civil authority to respect religious beliefs and the free exercise of these beliefs, and the fact that no person is less a citizen because of what he or she believes. Unfortunately, he also neutered the power of religious belief and trivialized religious faith by taking it out of the public arena altogether. His Catholic faith was no threat to the country because he stated that it had nothing to do with the real affairs of the country. "I believe in a President whose religious views are his own private affair," he told the assembled pastors after admitting that "it is apparently necessary for me to state once again – not what kind of church I believe in, for that should be important *only to me* (my emphasis) – but what kind of America I believe in." He said he wanted to be a Chief Executive "whose fulfillment of his Presidential oath is not limited *or conditioned by any religious oath* (again, my emphasis), ritual or obligation."

Does this sound like a person for whom his faith is his principal concern that integrates every other aspect of his life and which directs his every choice and action? Does this sound like a Catholic whose faith would "threaten or call into question the prevailing culture"? Not even close. According to his own words, President Kennedy saw his Catholic faith as having relevance only to him and no one else; he maintained that religious beliefs had no import beyond the individual, so much so that they had no bearing on issues or concerns that people of differing religious persuasions might share. In this view, religious beliefs bear no weight in public life. For President Kennedy, religion was irrelevant to economic and political life, a decorative extra that stood outside of what really mattered. He substituted "America" for any divine object of faith when he said, "it is necessary for me to state not what kind of church I believe in, for that should be important only to me, but what kind of America I believe in." Like most Americans, he failed to understand that beliefs are beliefs, and that any beliefs politicians carry into office, even if they might be classified as secular ones, should be as highly scrutinized as are explicitly religious beliefs.

Apparently, in the subsequent years of his presidency, when he sunk the country deeper into the Vietnam conflict, when he beat Russia at a game of nuclear chicken in the Cuban missile crisis, when he advocated lowering taxes, when he began to grapple with near apartheid in government schools, whatever he did "in fulfillment of his Presidential oath" was "not limited or conditioned by any religious oath, ritual or obligation." Would he have been a different President if he had allowed his Catholic faith to affect his policies? Did he sense that Catholic belief and practice, which at that time was fairly distinct, might conflict with some more generic values and goals in American society? We will never know. We do know that his political ambition caused him to muzzle his Catholic faith.

President Kennedy seemed to go out of his way to assure the clergy in Houston that his Catholic faith would not conflict with the dominant culture, that they needn't worry about his being Catholic because it wouldn't lead him to do anything that might upset the conduct of public affairs. John F. Kennedy even cozied up to the Protestant audience by pointing out that he voted against having an ambassador to the Vatican and voted "against unconstitutional aid to parochial schools."

Even though President Kennedy was later killed by an assassin's bullet, he did not die for the faith. Given the public diminishment of his faith in Houston, I doubt that he would have passed St. Edward's School's "soldier of Christ" standards.

In a curious way, there were two very different ways in which the Catholic Church of the late 1950's and early 1960's related to the country as a whole. On the one hand, the Catholic Church had a strong identity and was very distinct from the rest of America. On the other hand, Catholics wanted acceptance in this country and to "make it" in the dominant culture. These two contrasting states - distinction and similarity, separation and assimilation – and the tension between them need further examination.

CHAPTER TWO

IDENTITY AND LIKENESS

At 10:25 AM on Monday, October 2, 2006, Charles Carl Roberts IV walked into an Amish one-room schoolhouse in Nickel Mines, Pennsylvania with a 9mm handgun. Forty-five minutes later, four people were dead, including Roberts and three young schoolgirls; seven girls were wounded, two of whom died of their wounds soon after. The accounts of this incident and the days that followed are both horribly disturbing and truly remarkable. The oldest girls asked to be shot and the others spared. The families of the victims sought out the murderer's family to comfort them and to mourn with them.

The religious faith that was exhibited in Nickel Mines in 2006 was martyr-quality faith. Can we find among us a religious faith so deeply ingrained that youngsters will put themselves in front of others to be slaughtered? Can we find that sort of reflexive self-sacrifice anywhere? Do we often see the level of humility and mercy that would compel parents whose daughters were just killed to go to offer forgiveness to the murderer's family? Is it everyday compassion that invites the murderer's family to the Amish funerals and insists that not only funds be set up to assist the families of the victims but the killer's family as well? These things are uncommon indeed. But there they were for us to see in this peculiar group, the Amish. Values that are often preached about but rarely lived were evident in Nickel Mines, Pennsylvania in 2006. Goodness is more powerful than evil; "do not be conquered by evil but conquer evil with good," says the apostle. Forgiveness bears greater fruit than vengeance. Self-sacrifice is the cornerstone of the good life. Your eternal destiny is the end and goal that determines the many choices you make in life.

Ultimately, that is the bottom line. If the goal of your life is to be with God eternally, then your life and your death will be considerably different from having as your goals wealth, prestige, comfort, power, or fame. "Being in the world but not of the world," and, "setting your hearts on the things above," are central to the Amish way of life and, by the way, central to the life of any martyr.

Owing to the headlines and the news coverage, we all caught a glimpse into a different world. As if the pain of the violent death of their children was not bad enough, the Amish had to endure the secondary pain of intrusion. Into their world, removed by design from the rest of us, came the rest of us. Since most of my knowledge about the Amish is bounded by my recollection of that great film *Witness*, I had to do a little research to learn more. Christians, offshoots of the Mennonites, the Amish came to America from Switzerland in the 1700 and 1800s to avoid religious persecution in Europe. Intent on preserving their beliefs, culture, language, and customs, they keep interaction with the larger society to a minimum. With a prescribed and distinctive dress, they avoid much of what we accept as normal; they do not use automobiles, television, electricity they don't generate themselves, commercial chemicals, or gasoline. They do not go to school beyond the eighth grade. They promote the family and the community and not the individual. They are non-violent. While fierce about maintaining their way of life, they are not interested in converting anyone else to it.

They remind me of the Shaker communities that flourished for a time in the Northeast, utopian communities whose everyday lives were driven by their religious beliefs. Unlike the Amish, they were open to converts. The Shakers died out, though, because they made the mistake of insisting on celibacy for all members, not a good public policy for continuity.

The Amish – and there are different branches of the Amish scattered around several states and maintaining more or less severe lifestyles – are an even more distinctive group than was the American Catholic Church of the 1950's. Beyond keeping their own school system and language and rituals, the identity of the Amish is carved out in far greater detail than the Catholic Church ever thought of doing. In comparison with the Amish communities that are glaringly different from the rest of society, the Roman Catholic Church of the 1950s was barely perceptible against the backdrop of the prevailing culture. Given the distinctive features of American Catholicism in the late '50s, that's remarkable.

There is for every group, no matter its size, a relationship of similarity to larger more encompassing groups that defines or diffuses the boundaries of the smaller group, depending on the degree of likeness. The more different the smaller group, the sharper the boundaries; if the smaller group is similar to the larger group, the lines that distinguish the groups are less distinct. The smaller group either sticks out like a sore thumb or blends in so much that it goes unnoticed. The Amish are so unlike the rest of America; they are much more distinguishable from general American culture than even the Catholic Church of the 1950s.

An illustrative example of other types of distinct sub-groups or subcultures that quickly comes to mind is the familiar analysis of high school groups that breaks down the general high school population into the "jocks," the "preppies," the "brains," the "shop kids," the "goths" (or "hippies" or "beatniks" depending on the generation), the "4H types" and so forth. They all share some things in common in that they belong to the same age range, come from the same area, and attend the same school. Certain characteristics set the groups apart and these are usually dress, activities, lingo, and values to name a few. These traits tend to make the groups more or less distinct from the generic high schooler. Some groups are more different from the norm than others. If someone is walking the halls completely dressed in black with black eye makeup and a long overcoat, he or she will be noticed as different much more quickly than the basketball star in street clothes. They both belong to distinct sub-groups, but one's identity is more sharply drawn than the other.

Distinctions sharpen or lessen as identity is defined or blurred. It is easy to see this by examining ethnic groups and the process of their assimilation into the dominant culture. In the capital city of my home state, Providence, one of the larger ethnic groups that came to the city in the waves of immigration from 1880 to 1920 was the Italians. They came from villages and cities up and down Italy – a country, by the way, which barely had a national identity – and settled in this new place. They made a home but were not made to feel at home by those who were already here.

Like every other ethnic group, the Italians stuck together: in the North End, Federal Hill, and Silver Lake sections of the city. They kept the language; they had their own churches and civic organizations and credit unions. Some of the bakeries and sausage makers still exist today. By now, though, two, three, and four generations removed from the original immigration, the Italians do not stand out as distinctively as the newer immigrant groups in the city. Second, third, and fourth generation Italian-Americans enjoy Italian stuff by choice, not by nature. Out of curiosity or nostalgia, they eat Italian dishes and observe Italian customs but their main identity has shifted more to the "American" half of "Italian-American" and in the everyday course of events they resemble Polish-Americans and Irish-Americans and many other sub-groups in the American mix. For better or for worse, they have slowly become assimilated into American culture and have lost some of their identity along the way.

Through a series of everyday interactions, the ethnic groups blended. Tradesmen and factory workers left the ethnic ghettos to work and they mixed with other groups to do business. As soon as English was learned, ethnic identity was compromised. Ever so gradually, the interchange of cultures caused change: more radical for the smaller group and less so for the dominant group. The same is happening today with every other ethnic group. The more interaction is allowed or encouraged, the faster the process occurs. If very strict boundaries are maintained and contact is suppressed, the smaller group stays true to itself and the larger group remains unperturbed by the newcomer.

It must be remembered that the larger group is changed by the smaller as well. "Wednesday is Prince spaghetti day" was not a slogan meant for Italians. The rest of America was supposed to adopt this food. Every ethnic fraternal association will eagerly produce a list of contributions by their people to American culture. It might be foods or words or holiday traditions or business practices or religious customs or dress or any number of cultural accoutrements great or small. Whatever the influence, the larger United States culture has been changed by those it has absorbed. In that process of acculturation, if an ethnic group clung to its identity and remained very distinct, it had very little influence on the larger culture and became irrelevant to the everyday life of the majority. The more a sub-group related to the larger group and the more interchange they would have, the more likely the smaller group would affect the larger. But, as the smaller group's kinship with the larger group grew, it became more probable that the smaller group would lose its identity.

There is, then, a relationship between identity and likeness. They act as two poles between which the life of any subculture swings. If the group strengthens its identity, they are more alienated from the larger population. As they grow more like the dominant group, they lose their identity.

Returning to the Amish, the more an Amish sect is able to maintain a separation between them and American culture, the more they can be true to themselves. However, they will have little or no effect on the American way of life. If they accommodate the mainstream culture through commerce or tourism or any interchange at all, they will gradually begin to lose their distinctiveness and resemble the rest of us. Their way of life will come into question. For example, their odd notions about gender roles and education and worker productivity will be challenged. As their identity pays the price of cultural exchange, however, they may have a positive effect on American values as we admire and perhaps imitate their preference for simplicity, loyalty, and virtue.

Whereas the Amish have maintained a strong identity, American Catholics have not. They have shared the mindset of President Kennedy whose primary confession of faith was "I am an American," not "I am a Catholic."

Latin is no longer the American Catholic language. There are no more strict dietary customs. Distinctive devotions are either gone or largely unattended. While these might be considered mere "trappings," American Catholics might have a hard time naming substantive beliefs and practices that would distinguish them from the rest of American society. What is it, exactly, that distinguishes American Catholics from American non-Catholics?

Not much. Some would say that this is a good thing. They would say that the Catholic Church of the late 1950s and early 1960s was distinct but increasingly irrelevant. Traditionalists would argue that the Church has compromised too much. For older Catholics, that is a great debate to have.

One side would characterize the period following the early 1960's as one of decline for the U.S. Catholic Church. They would point to the numbers: the loss of priests and religious sisters and brothers, the drop in Mass attendance, fewer people going to confession, the closing of parishes, the disappearance of Catholic schools and hospitals. They would point to the growing and public dissension in the Catholic Church over birth control, married priests, women priests, and divorce. They would produce the many surveys about the opinions and lifestyle of Catholics and how they closely resemble those of American non-Catholics. They would ask, why? Why did the Catholic Church in the early 1960s deliberately seek change and plunge itself into an upheaval that would lead to atrophy?

At the beginning of the Second Vatican Council, the Bishop of Providence, Russell J. McVinney, who opposed extensive changes within the Church, was quoted in a national publication as saying of the Catholic Church, "Why change a winning team?" While more progressive Catholics might look at that remark and snicker, he wasn't delusional in making that statement. Into the early 1960s, the Catholic Church was booming in the United States as an institution. Seminaries and novitiates were bursting at the seams. There were parishes with two grammar schools running and simultaneous Masses in two or three locations to accommodate the crowds. Women's sodalities and men's clubs were thriving. It is possible to visit motherhouses of congregations of religious sisters and see buildings and chapels built in the late 1950s and early 1960s for several hundred sisters that have since been turned into nursing homes or community service agencies because there are very few sisters remaining. They and many urban parishes are the Catholic Church's version of western ghost towns that sprung up in the Gold Rush and were filled beyond capacity until the gold no longer panned out. So, Bishop McVinney was not necessarily a reactionary; he was raising a legitimate and almost obvious question, Why tinker with a winning formula?

There are plenty of answers to that question. The least satisfying ones say that Vatican Council II and the ensuing tumult were the work of the Holy Spirit. They recall the aged Pope John XXIII who surprised everyone by summoning the world's bishops to the Council, calling for an *aggiornamento*, the Italian word for revitalization or updating. He wanted to fling open the windows of the Catholic Church to let in sunlight and a fresh wind, an image that reached back to the Scriptures and the coming of the Holy Spirit upon the early Church. Perhaps the Vatican Council II was the work of the Spirit. Saying that is not informative enough, however. It is necessary to look at other reasons the Council was held, or to put it in religious terms, why the Spirit would have moved in that way at that time.

In those days, Europe was already entering a Post-Christian era. Having experienced and survived profound evil in the Second World War, Western Europe began taking the first steps into a different era, a different world, walking down a path that other parts of the world would, at some point, follow. Christianity, the caretaker and innovator of Western Civilization, was inadequate for the cultural, scientific, and sociological developments of the post-war world. Enshrined as a treasure of Western Europe, the Catholic Church was swiftly becoming petrified, irrelevant to the changing world. Not only did it not have the answers to the questions people were asking, no one was directing the questions to the Church anymore. Preserving the Catholic Church as it was and maintaining its identity was riskier in terms of safeguarding the Church than courting change as more and more people thought of the Church as a museum and not a vibrant system that equipped people to face the challenges of post-war society.

It may seem a bit removed as an analogy, but think of the major chains of video stores. They were home entertainment for years. They were huge and they were everywhere. Now, they are pretty much gone and they disappeared quickly. Why? Because they did not keep pace with technological change. Their product and service delivery simply became outdated. It is a faint comparison, but the lessons apply to any enterprise, the Catholic Church included. Post World War II, the leaders and thinkers of the Catholic Church, mostly centered in Western Europe, were reading the signs of the times and they saw a Church that would increasingly be pushed to the margins of people's lives and of world affairs. They saw a Church out of touch, removed from the reality of family life, of workers' lives, of the predominant cultural life, and they decided that *aggiornamento* was necessary if the Church was to survive.

Change was underway from the late 1940s onward. In 1943, Pius XII urged Catholics to read and study the Scriptures in their own languages. Tiny incremental changes were happening in the celebration of the Catholic Mass and Sacraments. Catholic Workers' movements were forming in Europe and the United States that brought Catholic thought and spirituality to solving social and economic problems. The Christian Family Movement was taking hold and injecting a revived Catholic perspective on marriage and family life. Even in the United States, Catholic thought was introduced to popular culture through Father Peyton's family prayer crusade and through the Emmy award-winning television shows of European-trained Fulton Sheen.

Change, then, had already started in the Catholic Church even before the Second Vatican Council. It was ignited largely in Europe by leaders who were looking into the future and not seeing an influential Catholic Church in their crystal ball, but it did not become a conflagration until it hit the tinder of societal unrest that was happening in Europe and the United States. It would be a mistake to think about the happenings in the Catholic Church apart from what was taking place in the rest of society. Revolution was everywhere, the result of a multitude of causes.

If you picture those two realities I mentioned above, Identity and Likeness, as opposite end points of a pendulum swing, as the 1960s played out, the pendulum for the Catholic Church in the United States began to swing away from Identity and toward Likeness. The Church made a conscious effort to become relevant and to speak in the language and culture of secular society. On a purely religious level, the Catholic Church dove into the ecumenical movement by which they sought common ground with other Christian churches and non-Christian as well. More and more of what made Catholicism distinctive was abandoned in favor of the common denominators of language and custom.

There are many who would say that all this change and upheaval has produced a better Church. They might characterize what has happened as separating the wheat from the chaff, and this "winnowing" has yielded a more informed and committed Church. One huge development over the last few decades is the blossoming of "ministries" within the Church and the expanding role of the laity. Years ago, the U.S. Catholic Church resembled a cruise ship. The bishops and the clergy were captain and crew and the laity were the passengers – along for the ride but not having any real role in the operation or navigation of the ship beyond paying for tickets. Now, the Church is more like one of those large sailing ships that people sign on to for "working vacations," paying to be part of the crew. Not only have lay people assumed liturgical roles, they fill administrative and service roles as well.

Additionally, the wisdom and mystery of the Church are more accessible through the use of the vernacular in the Mass and Sacraments, the proliferation of Bible studies and prayer groups, and the attendance at schools of theology by more lay people than ever before.

Those who argue that we have an improved Church would say that while the percentage of Catholics regularly attending Mass may be down at least those who attend go because they want to be there, not solely out of a sense of obligation. They would argue that Catholic religious observance has moved from being culturally determined to following from choice.

And so goes the debate about the changing Catholic Church post World War II. Regardless of the merits of the arguments or any judgments about winners and losers of the debate, one thing is clear. For better or for worse, the United States Catholic Church has swung from a distinct and easily identifiable institution and group of people to a Church that has blended quite well with the prevailing American culture. The forces of assimilation and the choices of Catholics have produced a mainstream Church.

If the Amish had undergone the same process, the elders among them would be mourning the loss of the soul of their religion. American Catholics, on the other hand, do not seem to mind that their church has become generic. While the U.S Catholic Church is becoming more like American culture and society, its identity is very much blurred.

Oddly enough, the Amish enforcement of strict separation from the rest of society and the U.S. Catholic drive to accommodate the rest of society spring from the same motivation: self-preservation. The Amish would not survive if they allowed themselves to mix with the non-Amish. The American Catholic Church would not have maintained its strength as an institution without jettisoning what was deemed old-fashioned and outdated and making itself more accessible to American society. Opposite courses of action on the Identity/Likeness continuum, but for the same purpose: survival, that is, to continue as a people and as an organization. This is what we see when contrasting the Amish and the U.S. Catholic Church. One reinforces peculiarity to remain separate and the other cultivates similarity to stay accessible. Both accomplish the same goal of self-preservation.

For American Catholics, is this the right direction? Is this what the U.S. Catholic Church ought to be doing? The answer to these questions depends on how one understands the purpose of the Catholic Church. Why does the Church exist? What is the Catholic Church supposed to be accomplishing?

CHAPTER THREE

THE PURPOSE OF
THE CHURCH

H oly Week – the most sacred time of the year in the
Catholic Church. Millions of Catholics meet to celebrate
what they consider to be the central mystery of life: death
and resurrection, the self-sacrifice of one man, his plea for everyone
to do the same. One Holy Week some years ago, I was working in
one of the most Catholic neighborhoods in one of the most Catholic
cities in the most Catholic state. There are more churches than liquor
stores in this neighborhood, not so much because of the number of
Catholics but because of the number of ethnic groups who could
not, or would not, mix. The neighborhood is changing, however,
and, although the majority of people are Catholics by Baptism, many
people are not going to church. More seriously, the neighborhood
was experiencing ethnic and racial tension and violence with the
influx of Hispanics, Asians and Black-Americans.

On a Monday morning I drove past the Italian church. One
would expect, at least some indication that this was Holy Week,
perhaps even a sign on the outside advertizing the times of the

services. There was a sign all right, but it said nothing about services. In fact, it said nothing about Holy Week. It loudly proclaimed the good news of a carnival to be held on May 1. All around the church parking lot and grounds, pennants with the colors of the Italian flag were flapping in the wind. No palms, no crosses, no liturgical colors. If a Hindu were brought before the church building that week and asked what the most prominent event was in the lives of the people of the parish, he would say very quickly, "A carnival on May 1."

The Irish church up the street wasn't any better. Parked beside the front steps of the church was one of those portable electric signs with the white backlit billboard and flashing yellow arrow. On it was a rather significant message for Holy Week: "Las Vegas Night - Dinner/Dance - April 24." One could only hope that the celebrants would turn off the flashing yellow arrow when they brought the Paschal Candle in.

On a main street of a neighborhood badly in need of hearing the Gospel, two Catholic churches during Holy Week used signs and decorations to hawk a carnival and a Las Vegas Night.

The Italian church was founded to service the many Italian immigrants who settled in that area. Although the parish continues services in Italian, there are very few, if any, recent Italian immigrants. The neighborhood itself has been chewed up by new roads and highways. Although a resident congregation still exists, the parish is really "home base" for second and third generation Italian-Americans who moved to nearby towns and suburbs. It could be argued that the parish exists more for them than the people who actually live in the neighborhood, as a kind of relic, a very expensive piece of nostalgia. It is very expensive because the parishioners recently refurbished the church and they operate a grammar school.

So, we have a parish whose main focus is preserving buildings and a school in order to service the past. It is not surprising that the focus of Holy Week would be a money-raising carnival that would also serve as a reunion for those who grew up in the parish. The interest is in maintaining the status quo. The energies are spent on keeping what already exists even if it does not address the needs of the neighborhood or include recent arrivals.

The Irish church was not as healthy. Its people left with the advent of the Italians and that was two or three waves of immigrants ago. The membership was dwindling, the building crumbling. Feeble attempts were made to minister to Hispanics but without any meaningful inclusion in parish life. The parish became irrelevant to the population it was supposed to serve and the response of parishioners and staff was predictable if lamentable: they continued to do what they always did. They continued to do what they knew best: hold dinners and dances for an aging population and former parishioners hoping that some money can be raised to make long past-due repairs to the Church. It didn't work. A few years later, the church was torn down and the parishioners melted away into other parishes or no parish.

There are thriving parishes, too. A survey of their activities would reveal well-populated religious education programs, services that feature good music and sermons that speak to the listeners, ministries to the bereaved, singles and divorced, strong commitments to charities and mission outreaches to third world countries, organized prayer and Bible study groups, youth programs that keep young people involved in the parish, major social events that are well-attended, and perhaps very meaningful service to people in personal crisis or difficulty.

Once you begin to bundle all that is happening in parishes – both the struggling and the bustling – with diocesan efforts in education, healthcare, and social ministry, there is a sense that the Catholic Church is still a going concern despite setbacks in numbers. Once all these activities are listed and even after it is noted that a great deal of good is being done, a basic question can and indeed, must, be raised: what is the purpose of it all? Why does the Church do what it does? Why does the Church exist?

It's a hard question to get your hands around. It's like asking, what is the purpose of the family? Why do families exist? You know there's an answer, but it seems like there are many acceptable answers and that the principal answer is too big or too mysterious to articulate.

I asked my daughters why the Catholic Church exists. Their fairly basic answer gave some guidance. "So that Catholics can be around other Catholics." There's a lot to unpack in that observation. There is more than the comfort felt in gathering with others who share a worldview and a set of beliefs. Catholics' being with other Catholics satisfies a need most everyone has to be validated in their self-concepts, that is, to have some reassurance that how they understand the world and their journey through life is not eccentric but, in fact, canonized by a long-standing tradition and a community of people who are invested in the same lifestyles and customs and aspirations. It is low-tech social networking, a loosely-organized chat room in which topics and vocabulary and etiquette are recognized and agreed upon.

From an individual's or family's point of view, the Church helps to reinforce organizing values that lend integrity and cohesion to that person or family. From the institution's standpoint, the family serves as a vehicle for minimal doctrinal education and strengthening of moral standards. From either perspective, congregants or hierarchy, a very high value is placed on formation. The classic example of this shared interest in formation is recalled in the war stories from Catholic school graduates who tell of being punished by the good sisters at school and then being punished a second time when they went home and complained about being ill-treated by the nuns.

These numerous purposes of the Catholic Church – deriving strength from numbers of people gathered around unifying principles; maintenance of an over-riding world view that reaches across time and cultures; the civilizing effects upon individuals, families and whole societies of doctrines centered on human dignity, fundamental virtues and redemption; accomplishing unparalleled works of education, healthcare, and public welfare – are not realized in thin air. They require a structure, an institution, buildings, a business organization, workers, money and assets that enable the Church to do what it does. It is like any other human enterprise in this way.

Whoever belongs to the Catholic Church becomes more by that membership. The Church is not unique in this; many other large organizations enrich their members in a variety of ways. Members of a vacation club or timeshare, for example, can greatly expand the options open to them by pooling property use and ownership with many other people. The reach of their single investment is widened tremendously by joining a timeshare. Similarly, by being a part of the Church the person is enlarged, for lack of a better word. Even the most insignificant Catholic touches something that stretches across time, channeling a collective wisdom that is the fruit of centuries and participating at least vicariously in an immeasurable scope of activity with locations in every part of the globe. Being Catholic means being identified with all of that; it is easy to see how Catholics are greatly enriched by their membership in the Church. This enrichment is also a purpose of the Church and begins to point toward the heart of the Church's reason for being.

In reference to the work of the Church, "enrichment" is a rather weak word. Enrichment may more properly be used to describe the benefits of belonging to Toastmasters International, or taking advantage of a continuing education program, or belonging to a fitness club. A more precise word for the effect of Church membership would be, "sanctification," rather than enrichment.

Sanctification. Making holy. That is a great deal more than "enrichment." It means participating in the divine. Sharing God's life. Not just imitating Jesus. Not just internalizing a code of ethics. Not just adhering to a body of doctrine. Not just becoming a better person by modeling oneself on Jesus and the saints. No, it is God dwelling within us. It is being transformed from within in our acceptance of God's saving acts.

Now we are stepping beyond the purposes of the Church that we mentioned above. We are crossing the great divide between the human and divine, between the time-bound and eternal, between the limited and the infinite. The Church is a human organization to be sure – all too human as I shall discuss later – but an organization that is graced, in which the Spirit of God breathes.

It is not too extraordinary to make this claim since one of the earliest images of the Church, used by St. Paul in the First Letter to the Corinthians, is the "Body of Christ." Jesus, fully human and fully divine as God Incarnate, lives in his Church. The Church, then, becomes an extension of the Incarnation and holds together these human and divine elements at the same time. This incarnational character is the great glory of the Church, but it is also the great scandal of the Church. Even with all the remarkable people and achievements, the history of the Church is also a record of hypocrisy. Every sin, every failing, every variance from the Church's true calling, stand as indictments of Catholics through the centuries, painful reminders that we have fallen short of the glory of God, that we are a people "on the way," pilgrims who have not arrived but who have enough hope to move forward, trusting that, at some point, we "might be made perfect even as your heavenly Father is perfect."

The Catholic Church, therefore, is a great deal more than an institution that organizes people to do good works. More than offering an integrative worldview or a culture that reinforces admirable values, the Catholic Church offers salvation. Consciously or unconsciously, people belong to the Church to be saved. Saved from eternal damnation. Saved for eternal life with God. Saved from brokenness. Saved for wholeness. Salvation.

But that's only part of the story. For the individual Catholic, being made holy, being saved is not an end in itself. The purpose of the Church is not simply to save you and me. Your and my sanctification is just an intermediate step, a first payment on the greater purpose of the Catholic Church. The Church doesn't exist so that Church members can improve themselves; self-improvement is not the principal function of religious experience or of church membership. Rather, it is the service of God's plan.

In the ancient story of Abraham God chose him and blessed him as a favorite, taken from all the people in the world as someone special in Gods eyes. As reported in Genesis 12: 1-4, God says to Abraham, "I will bless you and make your name great so that you will be a blessing. All the communities of the earth will find blessing in you." You can see that God's choice and blessing of Abraham were not done just for Abraham's sake; His favoring Abraham was not an end in itself. No, God was blessing Abraham so that through him everyone on earth would be blessed. In the same way, the sanctification that individuals find in the Church is not an end in itself. There is a larger and greater purpose for the Church and its members.

In 1975, when I was living the student life over in Europe, I traveled to Rome for Holy Week. Paul VI, a not very popular but probably a very good Pope (popularity and greatness don't always coincide), was pope at the time. I was an arrogant twenty-three year-old with sufficient nascent cynicism to be ready not to be impressed by the pope or by the sights of the center of the Catholic Church. Two things happened to me that Holy Week in spite of my interior posturing. One was a meeting with a seminarian studying in Rome who told me about his involvement with Mother Teresa's order, the Missionaries of Charity, and who gave me its address in London. This led me to contact the sisters and, within the next year, to work with them for the poor in London, an experience that taught me and continues to teach me a great deal about myself and about the spiritual life – what an unexpected and tremendous gift.

The other gift was walking over to the Coliseum on Good Friday for the Stations of the Cross. I have to reach for a cliché to describe the experience. I was a drop in the sea of humanity. People from every country on earth lined the streets and circled the Coliseum. Pope Paul VI, not an impressive-looking figure – in appearance a cross between a librarian and a banker – was driven through the streets acknowledging and blessing the tens of thousands of believers. On a small hill across from the Coliseum he carried a cross as prayers and meditations were read in several major languages. I felt a part of something greater than myself – the movement that stretched across the globe and the centuries in devotion to a man who died the death of a criminal, sentenced by the powers who ruled from the very city in which I stood. I was, at once, reduced to insignificance and, at the same time, made a part of a project of the greatest importance.

Being born in 1951, a baby-boomer and in training for the priesthood, I was given to introspection and a preoccupation with my personal growth. Standing in the crowd of Catholics outside the place of torture for the earliest believers and worshipping the Crucified One gave me perspective. I gained a sense that the spiritual life is not principally about personal growth and redemption; it is about something greater. Our individual spiritual lives exist in the context of a larger project. This "larger project" is the real purpose of the Church, and it was the writing of that same unimpressive pope that would articulate the reason for the Church's existence better than most.

In 1975, several months after I had seen him on that hill in Rome, Pope Paul VI issued a remarkable apostolic exhortation called "On Evangelization in the Modern World." In it, he very succinctly stated the mission and purpose of the Church:

> *Evangelizing is in fact the grace and vocation proper to the Church, her deepest identity. She exists in order to evangelize, that is to say, in order to preach and teach, to be the channel of the gift of grace ...*

He goes on to say what evangelizing is:

> *For the Church, evangelizing means bringing the Good News into all the strata of humanity, and through its influence transforming humanity from within and making it new: 'Now I am making the whole of creation new.' But there is no new humanity*

if there are not first of all new persons renewed by Baptism and by lives lived according to the Gospel. The purpose of evangelization is therefore precisely this interior change, and if it had to be expressed in one sentence the best way of stating it would be to say that the Church evangelizes when she seeks to convert, solely through the divine power of the message she proclaims, both the personal and collective consciences of people, the activities in which they engage, and the lives and concrete milieu which are theirs....

And he makes more precise this transformation of humanity:

... for the Church it is a question not only of preaching the Gospel in ever wider geographic areas or to ever greater numbers of people, but also of affecting and as it were upsetting, through the power of the Gospel, mankind's criteria of judgment, determining values, points of interest, lines of thought, sources of inspiration and models of life, which are in contrast with the Word of God and the plan of salvation."

Was this librarian/banker saying, "We want to overturn your society"? Sort of. These are not words that would normally be labeled "pious." They are not sentiments of a movement content to be inconsequential, decorative, or peripheral to everyday life. It is language with a revolutionary intent, impatient with the status quo. They are statements of an organization with an agenda, an outward-looking institution interested in growth and impact. Out of all the reasons for the Church to exist that one could list, Pope Paul VI was saying that "transforming humanity" is the central reason, the principal purpose that every other objective must serve.

Is the American Catholic Church accomplishing this mission? Is the Church that stands on the legacy of John F. Kennedy's

Catholicism being true to its purpose? Is the Church that once was peculiar more effective as the Church that accommodates? Is the Church that once braced its adherents for martyrdom now converting the nation by risking nothing?

While some may argue that the American Catholic Church lost members by becoming more relevant to American society from the 1960s on, more would say that the Church has been able to retain Catholics by adapting to a changing world. Regardless of the numbers, the question being raised is, has this embrace of being similar to the rest of America advanced the mission of the Catholic Church or has it served another purpose, that is, self-preservation?

Self-preservation is a healthy instinct for both individuals and groups. But the risk of dying is part of even the most basic life processes: cells die so that new ones may be produced, leaves fall from trees as a first payment on spring, animals put themselves in danger when they go out for the hunt. In the human world, everyone knows that the highest realms of spiritual life come from vulnerability and that no form of growth is possible without cutting the umbilical cord. Regeneration, progress, maturation require going against the instinct of self-preservation. "Gaining one's life by losing it" is the way one famous person put it.

Anyone who has made himself vulnerable knows that he would never find his true identity without doing just that. Ask any young person who made that big step of going out on her own. Ask any person who has honestly said, "I love you." Ask any couple who have had their first child. Ask any protester who has gone to jail for the first time. "Gaining one's life" means risking self-preservation. Successful groups and institutions can attest to the same truth. The alternative is inauthenticity. Survival, perhaps, but survival at a terrible cost. Attending to the self-preservation of the Church may result in abandoning its core mission of preaching the Gospel.

The primary instinct of the Church, then, should be "making the whole of creation new," not keeping itself going. Fulfilling its purpose of transforming the larger society forces a particular challenge on the Church. Being too peculiar may condemn the Church to complete irrelevance and render it incapable of delivering the message of salvation. Being too similar may rob the Church of the message itself: it will have nothing redemptive to say. That leaves the Church with the difficult task of maintaining an identity while remaining conversant with the prevailing culture. There is no settling once and for all time the question of whether one should cling to identity or be absorbed by a larger culture. The question must be repeatedly asked and provisionally answered in the everyday living of Catholics and the organized Church. The litmus test of success is what the interaction of the Church and American society yields. "By their fruits shall you know them" is a good guide. The mission acts as the standard and critique. Is the Church evangelizing? Is the Church "affecting and, as it were, upsetting, through the power of the Gospel, mankind's criteria of judgment, determining values, points of interest, lines of thought, sources of inspiration and models of life, which are in contrast with the Word of God and the plan of salvation?" Answering that question involves other questions: Is the Church being true to its message? Is the Church honestly living and proclaiming that message without counting the cost? Is the Church speaking to those who need to hear the message? To be mindful of its true purpose and to work effectively to accomplish that purpose require continual self-examination and constant correction. It is to this type of examination we now turn.

CHAPTER FOUR

RICH VS. POOR

In the July 1985 issue of Sojourners magazine I read a poem, reportedly written by a working-class Chilean woman shortly after President Allende was overthrown. This poem was so startling and direct that it stayed with me for a very long time. The story it told kept insisting on some awful and painful truths about the state of the Catholic Church even though the Church is never mentioned in the verses. The poem is entitled "Rich Woman, Poor Woman," and it begins this way,

I am a woman
I am a woman.

I am a woman born of a woman whose man owned a factory.
I am a woman born of a woman whose man labored in a factory.

I am a woman whose man wore silk suits, who constantly watched his weight.
I am a woman whose man wore tattered clothing, whose heart was constantly strangled by hunger.

I am a woman who watched two babies grow into beautiful children.

I am a woman who watched two babies die because there was no milk.

I am a woman who watched twins grow into popular college students with summers abroad.

I am a woman who watched three children grow, but with bellies stretched from no food.

But then there was a man;
But then there was a man;

And he talked about the peasants getting richer by my family getting poorer.

And he told me of days that would be better, and he made the days better.

We had to eat rice.
We had rice.

We had to eat beans!
We had beans.

My children were no longer given summer visas to Europe.
My children no longer cried themselves to sleep.

And I felt like a peasant.
And I felt like a woman.

The poem continues with these two voices from opposite sides of the economic spectrum telling of their experiences before, during, and after the power struggle in Chile. The poor woman details the drudgery and struggle of subsistence living she and her family experienced, the flash of relief with the provision of food and freedom, only to have it erased with the return of the ruling class to power. The rich woman begins with a description of a luxurious and carefree life, threatened briefly by the rise of leaders who began to insist on economic justice, but then restored by the counter-revolution. The poem ends with the old order restored:

> The beans have almost disappeared now.
> *The beans have disappeared.*
>
> The rice - I've replaced it with chicken or steak.
> *The rice, I cannot find it.*
>
> And the parties continue night after night to make up for all the time wasted.
> *And my silent tears are joined once more by the midnight cries of my children.*
>
> And I feel like a woman again.
> *They say, I am a woman.*

Reading through the poem is difficult but worthwhile. It makes the violence, injustice, and the intransigence of cruel systems very real.

I invite you to imagine the women in this poem and to wonder about their particular circumstances prior to the events described and how their lives may have intersected. One might wonder how closely they lived to each other or if they ever saw each other in their day's travels. Did the poor woman ever clean the rich woman's steps or try to peddle fruit to her on a busy street? Did the poor woman weave clothes that the rich woman passed over on the racks of the kind of store the poor woman would never approach? No one can say because the poem doesn't give that kind of information; one can only wonder.

You don't have to wonder if they belonged to the same church. You know. After all, this poem is set in Latin America where the vast majority of people are Catholic. A most horrible realization arising from this poem, then, is that these women are both Catholic – they may even light candles in front of the same statue. Perhaps within sight of each other in the pews, baptized from the same font, murmuring the same Creed. Yet, these sisters in Christ are economic and political enemies. Members of the Mystical Body, they are fighting to the death.

But use your imagination a little more. In your mind, broaden the picture beyond these two individuals. Imagine their neighborhoods and sections of the city. Now, there are many rich women and many poor women in the same parish, a parish filled with villas and shacks. Broaden the picture a little more and there are more rich women and more poor women in the same diocese, a diocese filled with overwhelming poverty and fabulous wealth.

Broaden the picture again and we are in it: First World Catholics and Third World Catholics. United States Catholics and Latin American Catholics (or African or Asian). Those who consume and those who are consumed. Those who measure their standard of living by the age of their appliances and those who live with no electricity. Those who consider themselves disadvantaged because they cannot renew their wardrobes and those who dress in rags. Those who live with modern means of transportation, communication, housing and medical care and those who cannot even dream of what we take for granted. Us and Them. Fellow Catholics, members of the same Church.

Is this the biggest sin? This glaring and purposeful inequality? I do not know. There are many possible nominees for the "gravest sin." The seven "capital sins" are strong candidates. Several instances of genocide and cruel exploitation also come to mind. For sure, all the sexual sins that are always preached against are small potatoes compared to these. I'm convinced that God doesn't really care too much about most of the sins we lose spiritual sleep over. All our breast-beating, confessing, and struggling about these sins tend to be convenient distractions from the real evil in the world.

The biggest sin? Who knows? Certainly this gap between the world's haves and have-nots and the misery it causes is up there. The wealth discrepancy between "us" and "them" is a scandal of the highest order, especially when both "we" and "they" are members of the same Church. The reasons for this shameful imbalance are covered by their complexity and magnitude but we cannot escape its indictment nor can we deny it. Not only are we reminded of it through the media and the ever-present appeals, our lives are also peppered with the fruits of the poor's labor in our clothing, food and fuel. We are spiritually tied to the poor because we follow the same Christ and perversely tied to them in an everyday posture of domination – a global wrestling match in which we have the poor gripped in a tight headlock.

How can this be happening? How can this be happening in an ancient worldwide Church founded on self-sacrifice, a Church that preaches compassion, identification with "the least," and a brotherly (and even sisterly) sharing of goods?

Poverty is, of course, relative to the standard of living in any given era and locale. My grandparents were among "the least" in their time and place. All of them immigrants - from Canada and Ireland and England – they came to live in the cities of Southern New England because there was work and the promise of a better life. I cannot cite figures because they are all dead and I never thought to ask, but they had no wealth and few assets, just some clothing and insignificant savings to keep them until they could find a job and then a place to live.

It was fairly easy to find work. The textile mills were humming along all the major and minor waterways of the mill towns. Even now, you can walk along the streets of Pawtucket and Woonsocket and Providence, Lowell, Fall River, and New Bedford through canyons of long mills. Silent now, they were once filled with workers and noises and smells that signaled commerce and prosperity. Through their willingness to work long and dull hours, my grandparents gained a foothold in the United States economy and society and began the generational mobility that pushed my parents and then me and my siblings and, now, my daughters upward. This story was duplicated by the millions across the United States, and the gap between rich and poor in the United States was filled in by a middle class that has stayed for sixty or so years. The future of the middle class is uncertain, but that is another story related to the shifting global economy, an economy that shares boundaries with the Catholic Church.

There is a museum in the northern Rhode Island mill city of Woonsocket called the Museum of Work and Culture and I went there to see the details of immigrant mill worker life from the early 1900's to 1950. I wanted to understand the day-to-day role these workers played in the ever-expanding northeast economy as well as the role the mill life played in the workers' lives. I mostly wanted to see where religion and the Catholic Church fit into their lives, particularly their economic lives.

The Blackstone River runs its southward route some fifty yards from the Museum of Work and Culture. Standing at the front door, one cannot see far because the view is blocked by the walls of brick factories that vie for space along the once cobblestoned streets. The slope to the river affords some view, and the most prominent building in sight, besides the succession of mill structures, is Precious Blood Catholic Church. Nearby are rows of brick houses where once lived many of the mill workers, often near to stores; both houses and stores were owned by the mill. Although there were several ethnic groups who came to Woonsocket during those decades of steady immigrant flow, it was mainly French-Canadians from Quebec who crowded into the city. Even the story of this one particular group is a fascinating study in shifting economies, stubborn clinging to ethnic and linguistic identity, antipathy between immigrant Catholics and Protestant natives, unionism, political power, and the cruel march of history. Some of what can be viewed at the Museum is peculiar to the Quebecois; much of it is can be applied to any immigrant group who made their way to the United States from the Old Catholic World.

They were Catholic that's for sure. But what difference did that make? More particularly, how did their Catholic faith help them in their poverty? They were poor. For these immigrants from Canada, life back in Quebec held no prospects. A farming economy had reached its capacity. The amount and quality of land could not sustain a growing population, and so over 900,000 Quebecois came to New England alone. They came without means or education; they came without skills. They came with families or joined them here after long train rides that sped them into another world: urban not rural; industrial not agricultural; diverse not homogenous; hostile not friendly. At least there was a chance to earn enough to survive.

Their government and Church up north were telling them not to go. They were warned that they would lose their culture and language and faith. They were told that Protestant mill owners would exploit them. They were told that they would never be accepted in American society. The Quebec officialdom was not completely off the mark. Life was hard. Tight living quarters; compensation that was better than back home but barely enough to pay off the mill owners for bringing them here by train, giving them a week of groceries, and apprenticing them on a machine that would be their constant companion. They worked from six in the morning until six at night six days a week. The textile mills were hot year 'round, and dusty and noisy with the continuous drone of the looms. Any breaks a worker took to go to the bathroom or get a drink or eat something cost them because they were paid by what they produced. And if they made a mistake or did something to the machine or interrupted the weaving of cloth, they could easily find themselves out on the street because trains brought new immigrants every day. Life was hard, but it was better than what they left and it got better still over the next few decades. How did their Church figure into this climb out of poverty?

The answer to that question is mixed. On the one hand, government and Church officials in Quebec were pulling on the wrong end of the tug of war that was economic transition to an industrialized and urban society. They even sent preachers across the border to exhort the ex-patriots to return home. Some did, but most stayed to forge a new life. Even as the factories prospered and the immigrants settled into being American workers, with every economic downturn and the predictable reduction of wages by the factory owners, many clergy urged their flocks to accept the lower wages because at least they had jobs. It's unclear if this was a fulfillment of Marx's indictment of a religion that promised happiness in the afterlife to justify suffering in the present or of more immediate financial factors. Pastors may have begun to align themselves with a prospering mercantile class who dropped steady contributions into the collection plate, a prosperity that would be threatened by worker unrest. Clergy may also have feared closures of factories and the disappearance of congregations, a fear that was not unfounded as the lifespan of textile factories sped past its highpoint and the mill buildings went silent one by one as the work went South.

On the other hand, the Church was a key to moving out of poverty. Three very concrete activities come to mind that were crucial to the immigrants' success. The first was education. Catholic schools gave the Quebecois children something they never had back home: an education. Even if that education was truncated because youngsters had to go to work, still, there was now a community investment in education and overall literacy rates and skills capacity began to grow. These early building blocks of an educated Catholic population would blossom a generation or two later after World War II when GI's took advantage of federal education aid to get college degrees and to move into professional careers.

A second factor was the Church's hands-on involvement in economic life through the creation of credit unions and the support of unions. Shunned by the non-immigrants and unable to build savings or gain credit, credit unions were formed by people through their association with the local churches. The first credit union in Rhode Island was formed by a French-Canadian group in the basement of Notre Dame Church in Central Falls. Through these small financial institutions, immigrants could buy houses, amass savings, finance businesses, and, thus, begin to build wealth. Along with the development of some financial muscle, immigrants also sought more power in the workplaces, and the Catholic Church was an ally. From the publication of Leo XIII's encyclical *Rerum Novarum* in 1891 that defended workers' rights and dignity to the union schools sponsored by churches in the 1930's that taught workers how to organize and why, the Catholic Church lent an imprimatur to unionism. This gave the American immigrant worker an authority and intellectual underpinning that did not depend on socialism or communism, ideologies that faced tremendous odds against their gaining a foothold in the American soul.

Above all, the Catholic Church gave the Quebecois and other immigrant groups a sense of worth. It wasn't just reinforcing ethnic identity by the preservation of language and customs. It was more the constant insistence by the Church on the dignity of the human person and the sanctity of each person because he or she shared in the sacramental life of the Church. Even if the greatest percentage of immigrants could not articulate these principles, they were in their genes, and their environment was soaked in the tradition that the value of each human being is not something that can be bought or owned or destroyed.

A strong argument can be made that the Catholic Church was instrumental in overcoming poverty for millions of Americans. The churches did not do this by becoming mirror images of the early Christians who "were together and had all things in common; they would sell their property and possessions and divide them among all according to each one's need." (Acts of the Apostles 2:44-45) Nor did the Catholic Church erase the divisions between the rich and the poor, the haves and have-nots in individual parishes or in any geographical area. The scandal of stark economic contrasts captured in the poem at the beginning of this chapter has also existed in the American Catholic Church itself. This failure to ease the economic hardships and sufferings of brothers and sisters in Christ, however, does not negate the powerful force the Catholic Church has been to bring about greater economic justice and the real prospects of a better life for many.

The Catholic Church has been most successful in this regard when it weds its lofty teachings with local and practical realities. The union schools are a good example. Not many parishioners are going to read *Rerum Novarum* or the more recent *Laborem Exercens* by John Paul II or *Caritas in Veritate* by Benedict XVI, but if they are gathered as a Church to grapple with the problems of everyday life in the workplace and the marketplace, they may experience how the Spirit is at work in their economic lives.

While there are more than enough examples of localized poverty that various waves of immigrants have faced at different times, the economic turmoil that is being felt in most places at the beginning of the twenty-first century is global. The Catholic Church is also global. Even the Quebec Church dared to cross national boundaries and attempt to reconcile divergent economic forces. Why cannot Catholics from different nations attack the disparity of rich and poor? Why cannot Catholics from different countries strike out on a different economic path? I don't mean relief work. I don't mean sending money to the mission lands. I mean Catholics who are bankers and investors and CEO's and economists and exporters; I mean the people who are making the global economy. Why cannot faculty of Catholic universities around the world investigate Catholic solutions to the gross inequality that plagues so many and the collateral suffering that is taking place as economies rise and fall in a shifting world order? The wisdom is there. The worldwide reach is there. Many of the economic actors on the global stage are Catholics. Why isn't there a movement of Catholic economic practice?

There are more than enough encyclicals and pastoral letters and council documents from the popes and bishops and theologians.

Eradicating the disparity between rich and poor and ending the exploitation that is tolerated and overlooked daily is the mission in which the laity should shine. But it's not happening. The mechanics of the global economy grind on, seemingly unaltered by the Catholic Church or any faith, and thought by most to be unalterable as if how value is created and distributed is a spiritually and morally neutral process that abides by its own laws, and only those laws apply. Introducing alternate ends and means or different metrics into "neutral" economic systems is considered illegitimate. For Catholic entrepreneurs and investors, introducing faith into finance is too risky; playing by different rules invites failure.

Does Catholic faith have a place in corporate structures, balance sheets, and investor returns? Many American Catholics would say, no. Along with many other parts of the American culture, American Catholics have assimilated an insistence on the marginalization of religious faith that prevents them from allowing any meaningful role for religious belief in the everyday affairs of commerce. This exile of religion from the worlds of business and politics in the United States is well-addressed in Ann Douglas' scholarly work, *The Feminization of American Culture*, in which she details the transformation of traditional American Protestantism into liberal Protestantism, a period during which she claims that women and clergy lost their role in economic and political life and decision-making, thereby becoming decorative and inconsequential. Her thesis goes on to view this development as a precursor to modern consumer culture in the United States with women and sentimentality at the heart of that culture, but her first insight is what is of most importance for our discussion. Women and religion are at the boundaries, standing on the sidelines while men play the real game unfettered by feminine or religious concerns.

A couple of incidents from parish life may help illustrate this diminishment of the power of religion. I was assigned as a deacon to a suburban parish right out of seminary in 1978. Attending my first parish council meeting, I was a little wide-eyed because there was a heated discussion about whether or not the American flag should be placed in the sanctuary. The associate pastor cited bishops' documents directing that national symbols such as flags should never be a permanent fixture in a sanctuary because the Catholic Church was a universal church with no national boundaries. Some parishioners saw this as unpatriotic and disrespectful of the liberties enjoyed in this country and preserved through the sacrifices of veterans. The other side countered that our freedom and dignity did not come from any government. And so the argument went with tempers rising and sensitivities bruised. Who knows if the clergy were tyrants or prophets, but the flag stayed in the choir loft at the rear of the church. I did not say a word, but just sat, took it all in, and tried to remember if and when this aspect of parish life was treated in my seminary training.

Five years later, I was the associate pastor in that same parish and by that time I was talking. Parish priests around the United States were instructed that Advent season to preach about the U.S. Bishops Conference's Pastoral Letter titled *The Challenge of Peace*. It was an analysis and critique of the nuclear arms race and the role of the United States in it. I really don't know how many priests actually preached on that document for the four Sundays of Advent, but we did – without the flag in the sanctuary. Parishioners walked out – not in great numbers, but enough to be noticed. They spoke with me afterwards to express their displeasure and to make the point that the bishops should stick to "spiritual things" and stay away from foreign and military policy. They had no business meddling in those spheres, the parishioners observed, and they further noted that people did not come to church to hear about these sorts of things. In the end, we all sort of agreed to disagree about the province of the Church's teaching mission.

Looking back, I am struck by the fact that some of the same people who argued to have the flag in the sanctuary insisted with the same passion that faith and political affairs should not mix. It was a perfect illustration of what Ann Douglas had written about, that Americans allow religion to play an emotional role that makes people feel better – in this case, to shore up patriotism – but would wall off religion from any role that might have a real effect on the affairs of the day. Religion is reduced to fashion, an object of personal preference, the result of whim, fancy, opinion, or private experience, but it is not in the company of objective reality or hard fact. Religion and religious concepts are often used by politicians and business people, but only in jingoism or ad campaigns, not to make decisions, advance policies, or map out fiscal strategies.

Remember, this flare-up in the parish was about the Catholic Church preaching on war and peace, subjects about which there is a long tradition of teaching in the Catholic Church. Imagine if the preaching had turned to economics or finances or business. Even though the Catholic Church has taught extensively about these things as I have noted, there would be even less stomach for blending religion and money than there was for religion with war and peace.

This divorce between religion and politics or religion and economics that is a reality in American life has become codified in the popular notion of the separation of church and state, a handy if elastic concept used to legitimize keeping faith and commerce apart. American Catholics have accepted this postulate and, like most Americans, have used it as a sort of spiritual electric fence to maintain strict boundaries between the sacred and the secular.

This demarcation is almost too convenient, an excuse to leave lifestyles and economic systems unperturbed. Of course, Americans are not alone in doing this; the fact that the world of business and finance remains untouched by faith is not peculiar to the United States. Other countries and cultures also manage to compartmentalize their economies so that the have's have and the have-nots don't and religious belief and practice have little impact on that economic status quo. Other countries have other excuses or rationales for making sure that religion doesn't interfere too much with business. In the United States, however, religion has been marginalized, even trivialized, and so is kept at the outskirts of public life.

If American Catholics keep their faith away from how wealth is created, amassed, expended, and distributed, there is little opportunity for martyrdom, little chance of witnessing to other values, little possibility of challenging or changing the status quo.

Without a doubt, there are millions of financial decisions made by American Catholics motivated by faith; tremendous acts of generosity, countless sacrifices made for others, selfless sharing of resources. The overall economic life, however, remains unconverted, unmoved, and inequalities such as those portrayed in the poem at the beginning of the chapter remain.

CHAPTER FIVE

AUTHORITY

"Authority" is a difficult word. It's a difficult word for teenagers, as it should be; it's difficult for baby-boomers, as it must be for those who grew up post-World War II in the shadows of evil and the insecurity of the nuclear age. In the digital age, it has become, for most, a complicated word. How people regard the authority of coaches and teachers and parents and elected officials and many more "people in authority" is changing rapidly. It is no different in religious organizations. People's understanding of "authority" and how it functions in their lives is at the heart of the struggle within the Catholic Church, particularly in the United States.

Before laying out some thoughts about authority and applying them to the state of authority among U.S. Catholics, it is important to distinguish between authority and power. Both authority and power elicit responses of either obedience or disobedience, but authority and power are very different. The reaction to authority is a free act of assent, an acknowledgment that the person or the directive can be trusted as truthful. The reaction to power does not involve freedom or recognition of truth. The difference between the effects of authority and power is the difference between cooperation and coercion, respect and fear.

We are speaking here of authority, not power. Power and one's relation to power is simple and mechanical. Understanding why people follow someone who has power over them is not difficult. Knowing why people recognize a person, organization or teaching as authoritative is.

On conscious or unconscious levels, people live according to some authority all the time. As much as it is preferable to live according to what we *know* to be true, which requires only the authority of proven fact, there is so much that we do not know or that is unknowable that living according to what we *believe* to be true becomes inescapable. That's where authority comes in. In matters small and large, we live according to what we accept on some authority. In order to help unwrap the notion and experience of "authority," I have been thinking back on statements that I accepted as authoritative at different moments throughout my life and that have stuck with me and continue to shape my life because they still carry credibility for me.

"God has given you talents and he expects you to use them."

I grew up in a family of seven children. We were a religious family. There was a Scripture passage to which my mother referred often and it is emblematic of my upbringing. The passage was Matthew 25: 14-30, the parable of the master who gave his servants money to invest. At times when my mother was reflecting on our conduct or our performance in school or our life's ambitions and dreams, she would say, "God has given you talents and he expects you to use them." I believed her. I still do. Why?

She was my mother, first of all. Simply being in that central role gave her authority. Trust blossoms or withers in the dynamics of this fundamental relationship. If a person learns to trust at all, that's where it happens. A mother's authority is *a priori*, a given, and although her influence and credibility will subsequently be tested and diminished by the child's maturing, experience, and freedom, as well as competing authorities, there will always be a certain divine right attached to a mother's rule, perhaps even more so than that of a father. It was no different for me and, in the case of this particular pronouncement by my mother, she was quoting Jesus from the Scriptures which doubled the power of this statement.

"It doesn't matter what job you do as long as you are happy."

One of my grandmothers told my sisters not to whistle because girls whistling made the Blessed Mother cry. My other grandmother taught them how to whistle. She was the grandmother who would say, "It doesn't matter what job you do as long as you are happy." I grabbed hold of that statement as true when I was a kid. Another fifty or so years later, there is still a truth inside of it that instructs me. On the surface, saying, "It doesn't matter what job you do as long as you are happy" is silly. Many would say that your happiness is, to some degree, contingent on your job. Don't people look to their jobs to bring them some satisfaction? Don't they want their jobs to provide sufficient income for their families? My grandmother, however, wasn't talking about surface realities. She was reaching beyond the authority of the conventional, going beyond the evident to point to the phenomenon that our happiness is, at some point, disconnected from our activity, our status, or our earning power, that our self-worth is grounded in something deeper. The authority of the statement was derived from challenging commonly accepted wisdom.

"Confronting a person directly invites a lie."

Sister Walter Marie, RSM was a wonderful fifth-grade teacher, much loved by her students. Recalling her is an antidote to all the horror stories about nuns in Catholic grammar schools. She would read to us, sometimes for a half hour to forty-five minutes at a time, from biographies of saints and Catholic heroes and heroines, and the class would listen and be captivated. She taught all the subjects flawlessly and I don't remember her raising her voice. I found out years later that we were her first class. I also learned that during that year – it was the 1962-1963 school year – her sister fell ill and died. Those were the days when religious sisters were not allowed to go and come as they pleased or needed, and so I believe that she experienced her sister's illness and death for the most part separated from her family.

I don't remember the details of an incident that happened during that year, but another classmate said something about me that was not true and my intention was to confront her to see exactly what she said and why. Somehow, Sr. Walter Marie heard about this possibility and she came to me and suggested that I not do that because my pressing the classmate about what she said would likely cause her to lie. I followed her advice and have since been conscious of balancing my own needs with others and being aware that by narrowly focusing on what I consider a good may actually cause a greater evil. Sr. Walter Marie's authority came from my recognition that she was seeing the larger picture and had a wider good and larger value in mind than I did. I also think her suffering, hidden from us but still a part of her daily life, lent her words and person authority.

"Your body never lies."

It was a course I took in my sophomore year of college. I will not identify the professor because this sentence, "Your body never lies," is the only thing I remember from this class and the professor deserves better than that. When he made this comment as an aside during one class, I didn't accept it right away although I knew at some level that it was true. It took a couple of years of thinking about it and observing how it applies before I believed this saying. Part of the truth of it lies in a belief in the unity of our bodies and our spirits and in the wonder at the simplicity of such a barometer for what is good or harmful to us. The authority of the statement developed; it did, indeed ring true, but its authority grew over the years of testing it against experience or, better, testing experience against that dictum.

"No train is worth running after."

The four years I lived in Belgium, I did not own a car. Travel in the town was on foot; trips of any distance were done by train. A few times in a row, I found myself running with friends across train station plazas and platforms to catch trains that were maddeningly on time. One day, I stopped running and walked deliberately while pronouncing to the others, "No train is worth running after." At the time, I was in graduate school and seminary formation, chasing after a vocation, working for grades and a degree, following priestly training through which people progressed because of favorable evaluations of performance and attitude. It's no wonder that I was struck with the thought that "no train is worth running after." The statement is, of course, false. There are, in fact, "trains" worth chasing, goals that deserve our going all out, without reserve and at full speed. The truth of my pronouncement lies in it's being a limit, a boundary, a critical standpoint from which life's goals and activities can be assessed. The underlying insight that stayed with me is that since there are few things in life that are worth running after make sure that what you are chasing is among them.

"Scratch where it itches."

A good friend of mine who is still a priest, and a wonderful one at that, once told me three rules of community life that had been passed on to him. He was educated by Benedictines so maybe they come from that oral tradition. The second and third rules are, "Never volunteer for anything," and "If you are asked to do something, never refuse." The wisdom of those rules for community living is not as easily discerned as that of the first rule, which is "Scratch where it itches." When I first heard this quote, my reaction was the same as all the folks' to whom I've repeated it: recognition that it is true. If someone has wronged you or rubbed you the wrong way or if you have a problem with that person, do not go to other people to complain or gossip. Either remain silent or go directly to the person to hash it out straightforwardly. The rule's authority comes from centuries of community living, experience gained, shared, and tested over generations.

"If God wanted someone else to do this job, he would have called someone else."

Back in 1977, I was ordained a deacon in the local parish church in Leuven, Belgium, where Damien the Leper, St. Damien of Molkai, is buried. A bishop, who was a chaplain in the U.S. military, was the ordaining prelate. I do not remember his name, but I do remember what he said to us. He observed that we - those to be ordained that morning – might be feeling inadequate, that we might be thinking that we are not good enough preachers, or that we do not know enough theology, or that we are not holy enough. The bishop told us that "if God wanted someone with other qualifications, someone else to do this job, he would have called someone else. But He didn't. He chose you." It was a real admonition to trust the call; trust the call not because of some feeling that we had but because the call had come over a long period of time and through many channels: parents, families, teachers, friends, other believers, spiritual directors, seminary faculties, communities of faith whom we had served, our own bishops, and as a small part of that, an inner attraction to follow what we had been asked to do in so many ways and through so many means. What the bishop said was an authoritative statement about recognizing the authority of vocation.

Frederick J. Sneesby

"My vocation is love!"

Parish priests are expected to go on an annual spiritual retreat. Usually, a formal retreat will be presented to groups of diocesan priests (priests who work for a diocese and not for religious orders like the Franciscans, Jesuits, Dominicans, etc.), but in 1984 I went by myself to a retreat house in Gloucester, Massachusetts, a property owned by the Jesuits overlooking the Atlantic Ocean. I don't remember why, but I had brought along, *Story of a Soul: the Autobiography of St. Therese de Liseux*, the book written by St. Theresa, a young French woman who joined a cloistered convent and died in 1897 at the age of 24 after an uneventful life. The book was published the year after she died and became a spiritual classic that led millions around the world to learn about this saint and the way of life she advocated, what she called the "little way." For her, the measure of life is not how much one accomplished but with how much love one acted, even in the simplest of activities like cooking for one's family or going to work each day. Her "little way" put holiness within everyone's reach.

I spent the three or four days at the retreat house in silence, resting, sitting in the chapel praying, and reading *Story of a Soul*. It is not an easy read in that the language is highly stylized religious language from the late 19th century – and I was reading it in an English translation of the French – with imagery and expressions that almost offend with their sentimentality and effusiveness. Nevertheless, I was reading it and came to Chapter IX, the chapter about her vocation along with her reflection on the thirteenth chapter of Paul's First Letter to the Corinthians ("If I speak with human tongues and angelic as well but do not have love, ..."), the place in the book in which she exclaims that she has discovered that her "vocation is love!" I re-read sections of the chapter, dwelling on sentences like "He has no need of our works but only of our love," and meditating on the words of Paul about the emptiness of religious life without love.

I believed what these words were saying not as random spiritual axioms but in direct reference to my life. I knew that I was empty, and my life began a change that led, I believe, to my leaving the priesthood five years later and eventually marrying. The authority that I invested in these words came from how revelatory they seemed to be for me to understand my self and my life. This sort of experience of authority is fraught with danger because it flirts with delusion. It is equally risky to ignore its message.

"For the measure you measure with will be measured back to you."

There are many sayings from Sacred Scripture that I could list, I guess, but if I had to choose one to frame and hang on my office wall, it would be this one, Luke 6:38. It is authoritative, first of all, because Jesus said it, and so belief in his being God incarnate and the trust and reliance I have in him carry into these words. The depth of this saying's authority cannot be any greater, then, but its authority also has a breadth because it proves itself true over and over again not only in the lives of believers but for unbelievers as well. It is a minimal statement of justice and, at the same time, an invitation to expand our virtue. It is both a warning and a promise. It portends both punishment and reward. It is common sense, but inspired.

These nine statements, their contexts and impact, and why they were authoritative for me, demonstrate some elements that are useful in understanding authority. First of all, a person may carry authority by virtue of his or her role, like mothers ("God has given you talents and he expects you to use them"). That role may be woven into some social fabric, like parents, and the fact that the person fulfilling that role has authority is accepted without much thought. Or, it may depend on a more deliberate group designation, like a public official, or an umpire in a baseball game. Authority that is embedded in a role is not everlasting or unchangeable. Over time, it may erode due to different causes, or, it may shift from being absolute to conditional authority. The advice a parent gives is received much differently by a son or daughter on the other side of adolescence, but it will always carry weight.

Still remembering what my grandmother said ("It doesn't matter what job you do, as long as you are happy"), it seems that seeing beyond the superficial or conventional carries authority. Challenging the evident is not enough, by itself, to be authoritative, otherwise anyone or anything idiosyncratic would be believed. There has to be an accompanying awareness of the inadequacy of the conventional and a subsequent confirmation – usually by experience – that the uncommon insight brings one closer to the truth of things.

Sister Walter Marie's saying "Confronting a person directly invites a lie" drew authority from two sources. First of all, it invoked a wider perspective that demands of any reflective person an acknowledgement of his or her limitations; he or she may not see it all, know it all, or have captured all possible wisdom, and so ought to give way to the broader view, the larger picture. Sister Walter Marie also held authority because she had suffered. Suffering strips away pretense, posturing, illusion, and apparent truths. It fashions character, will, and virtue in the workshop of humility. Great deference is given to one who has suffered and what that person brings to the rest of us.

Having heard the professor say "Your body never lies" and knowing that it only rang true for me after years of considering it alongside my experiences tells me that the authority of a statement or a person many times needs our experiences to move us from reserving judgment to being assured, from suspicion to certainty. This happens a lot with instruction we receive (usually unsolicited) as young people. Many times if we recall something an adult said to us years ago and it resonates in our present experience we find ourselves thinking "Now I know what he meant," or "It didn't mean anything to me then but now I see."

As I wrote, "No train is worth running after" is false but it still is authoritative. Like any extreme statement, it pushes us to purity and challenges us by its claim to absoluteness. By searching for and finding the instances in which it is false, we find the truth buried inside. In this case, the truth is that the degree of our effort must match the worth of the cause. Does the goal deserve our investment? The authority of extreme statements like this comes from their ability to insist that we find the truth. In this way, they have both the power and shortcomings of adolescent idealism. Somewhere in the ideal – too rigorous to align with real life – is the call to our better selves.

The authority behind "Scratch where it itches" and "If God wanted someone else to do this job, he would have called someone else" is what I would call "retail authority" because it draws its influence from the many and the consistent. When a variety of voices is saying the same thing or when something is accepted as true over a long period of time, it carries a great deal of weight for the individual. In some ways, this brand of authority resembles the authority gained from the wider perspective or from the test of experience mentioned above. Another example would be the common maxim "Honesty is the best policy." So many different kinds of people have found it to be true and to have beneficial effects in their lives, and so many groups have adopted it as a reliable guide to the good life, and so many generations have preserved and lived this practical rule, that it carries a great deal of authority going forward.

The last two sayings – "My vocation is love!" and "For the measure you measure with will be measured back to you" – and their sources are much trickier to consider than the others. Sensing an authoritative word for one's life such as I did on that retreat in 1984, or ascribing divine origin to a saying is like walking a tightrope without a net. It can be disastrous. There is so much opportunity for delusion or illusion; there is a great temptation to choose the convenient or agreeable; it offers too easy of a route to validation or affirmation. These sorts of experiences of inspiration dwell in the same world as our experiences of conscience. We hear an inner voice; we feel a compunction; we gain an insight through no effort of our own; we are shown a direction without seeking it; we know right or wrong without looking it up somewhere; we gain new knowledge without asking a question; we are moved to write a song or compose a poem; we have a breakthrough in research; a new proposal for work gels; there are all sorts of similar experiences that have mysterious origins. They are experiences we cannot deny but have difficulty explaining. They carry the authority of sensory experience but with a question mark: are the lessons carried within these experiences really true? Are they something upon which we can really rely? The answer to those questions is supplied by the other sources of authority that I have outlined. What has come to us from beyond ourselves needs to be validated by experience and suffering, by the communities to which we belong, and by the test of time. All of it works together to tell us that what presents itself as authoritative can be believed, trusted, and relied upon.

From the above examples it is evident, too, that whatever holds authority for us is a matter not just of its content but also of its source. In other words, as important as it is for each person to know the answer to the question what do I believe? a more important question, perhaps, is whom do I believe?

In large measure, American Catholics are not believing bishops and those clergy and laity who share in their teaching and governing ministries. The Catholic Church in the United States has been suffering a rolling crisis of authority for a few decades now. There are more scholarly and insightful works than this one to which readers can refer for a deeper and broader understanding of what has happened in the last fifty or so years. For our purposes, I want to discuss three causes of this continuing crisis.

Back in the 1960's, when the fault lines of generations and culture were shifting and during the quakes and aftershocks of that decade, many people either had difficulty standing or else could no longer find the spot on which they used to stand. The Catholic Church was examining its teaching on artificial birth control, a recent development in medicine at the time. Touching on the subject in general terms during the Second Vatican Council, the

Council Fathers began to sketch new moral foundations for married sexual life by broaching the concept of "responsible parenthood" (see *Gaudium et Spes*, 49-51) even as they required obedience to the Church's teaching authority on the regulation of birth. The Council Fathers went no further; instead, with Pope John XXIII, they established a papal commission to study the moral issues surrounding artificial birth control more deeply. This commission survived John XXIII and the Council itself, finally sending a report with recommendations to Paul VI in 1967. Paul VI did nothing as a result of receiving this report until June 1968 when he published the encyclical *Humanae Vitae*. Paul VI did not follow the lead of *Gaudium et Spes* with its moral model of responsible parenthood, instead opting to reiterate the condemnation of artificial means of birth control based on traditional natural law teaching.

Given what was happening in Western Europe and the United States to many institutions as well as cultural and moral norms, Paul VI's decision to promulgate *Humanae Vitae* was prudent. He did not want to abandon the natural law underpinning of the teaching on artificial birth control for fear that the whole range of sexual moral teachings would then fall. Why add additional torque to the forces of societal change that were shaping a new world? Paul VI could not be expected to foresee how much *Humane Vitae* had the opposite effect from what he desired. Instead of shoring up Catholics' understanding of and adherence to the Church's teaching on birth control, it released an avalanche of questioning and protest and the eventual rejection of this teaching by the majority of Catholics and many clergy. Disciplinary action against dissenting theologians was like trying to cap the lamp after the genie got out. No matter how many times the pope and bishops repeated and explained this teaching, there was no turning back the clock or reversing the consequences of taking this stand on artificial birth control.

With *Humane Vitae* and the ensuing controversy, the teaching authority of the Catholic Church was substantially damaged and has never recovered. Theologians and clergy alike knew that the teaching was questionable from a theological perspective. Lay Catholics knew the teaching was suspect from their experience, and this discrepancy between what they knew from experience and what the teachers of the Church were trying to sell as authoritative was too wide to ignore.

The second crisis of authority was already underway even before *Humanae Vitae* except nobody acknowledged it. We know now from the testimony of thousands that, at least going back as far as the memory of the living can reach, children were being sexually abused by clergy – not just a few, not in isolated instances, not as anomalies in otherwise chaste priestly lives. No, the number of victims is unknown; the abuse was widespread and often perpetrated by serial abusers with scores of victims each.

We now know that this abuse was woven into the fabric of Church life. Abuses must have been known not just by superiors and bishops but also by fellow clergy, rectory staff, adult leaders in parishes and schools, police, counselors, and even parents who joined the great silence that allowed the abusers to go unpunished and the abuse to continue. It is clear that in diocese after diocese, the interests of the institutional Church were chosen over the welfare of children. Even after cases of abuse were brought into court through civil suits, the Church would stonewall trials and employ available legal devices to avoid taking responsibility and dealing honestly with what had happened.

Both the abuse and the cover-ups have been reprehensible; they are two sides to one scandal: the Church living a lie. "I am here to lead parishioners to holiness by word, sacrament and example" was really, "I am here to satisfy my own needs and drives." "The Church is the sacrament of salvation" was cover for "The Church is an organization with assets to protect and an image to uphold." The priestly class ordained for service was really a priestly caste with its own culture and rules and privileges, an insular cohort whose isolation has been preferred not just by bishops and clergy but also by most lay Catholics. This lie has, of course, called into question the preaching and the teaching, the causes and works of the Catholic Church.

One feature of online news is the ability for readers to submit and see comments about articles. If there is an article concerning the Catholic Church's taking a stand or making a statement about current culture or practice, public policy or government action, it is almost guaranteed that many of the subsequent comments will say something to the effect that the Catholic Church ought to take care of its own troubles first before offering advice to others, or that the Catholic Church has a nerve to take anyone to task after allowing its priests to assault children. Because the Catholic Church lived a lie, because the Catholic Church betrayed the trust of its people, because the Catholic Church hid the crimes of its officials, its standing to preach and teach and lead has been diminished, its moral authority choked.

Between these two events, the publication of *Humane Vitae* with its consequent controversy and the sexual abuse scandals along with the cover-ups, the Catholic Church's teaching and moral authority have been severely damaged. And now, as if having the Church's authority weakened on these two fronts weren't enough, we have also entered an age in which the whole notion of authority is being shaken and changed everywhere in society, not just in religious matters. Much of it has to do with how people access and share knowledge and experience in the digital age.

In July 1993, when the Internet was becoming something the public could join, there was a magazine cartoon by Peter Steiner in *The New Yorker* that pictured two dogs sitting in front of a computer. One dog was saying to the other, "On the Internet, nobody knows you're a dog." It wasn't so much a comment on the anonymity (swiftly disappearing) of Internet use, but an insight into the democratization of communication and knowledge sharing. Publication and broadcast and mass communications are no longer in the hands of a few but within reach of the many. Access to knowledge – even highly specialized knowledge – has been thrown wide open. The sharing and validation of experience through the Internet and, now, various social media, has a scope and an immediacy that are entirely new. Zillions of transactions are done remotely, somehow capturing the confidence of a handshake without personal contact.

What does this mean for authority? It is acquiring new meaning. You say you're an expert? I can find what you know. You say you're a specialist? I can read the journals sitting on your bookshelves. You're a teacher? Or a coach? I'm not sure what I need you for anymore. How should I plan a career? Let me consult ten blogs and twenty sites. I don't know what to make of my reaction to marital stress? There are hundreds of people I can find who have had similar experiences. Security, firewalls, and encryption are the new pillars of society as they protect our exchanges. Hits and views and followers are signals for someone or something to take note of. Reputation and ratings have become the trust currency of trading. Probability, the chance that you will get what you're looking for in goods or advice, is the new gauge for credibility. There are whole sites whose sole purpose is to assure users that they can rely on certain products and services.

Are the Internet and social media just more proving grounds for those who would claim authority? Or do they make those in authority presumptuous, even irrelevant? It's tough to be a leader when your listeners are "googling" your statements as you make them. It's hard to be a preacher when there are hundreds of millions of pulpits. It's hard to engender faith when thousands of friends and followers will send prayers or "Amens" instantly to those in need.

The good news is that so many are now empowered, able to gain somewhat equal footing to standard arbiters of truth or traders in goods and services. There are so many more seekers who can expect to find what they're looking for. The bad news is that with at least an equal number of people who claim to have answers to questions and needs, the rate of failure and disappointment will eventually lead to a rise in confusion and skepticism. The explosion in the availability of knowledge will vastly increase the need for discernment and wisdom.

Whatever the future course of this revolution in access to information and the sharing of experience, it represents a time of crisis for authorities, including Church authority. How Catholics conceive of and exercise and respond to authority is changing, ready or not. This is a disturbing development to an organization that has been suffering from a lingering crisis of authority, as described above. For a community of faith, there can be no greater threat than a crisis of authority. If those who would recommend to the members of the Church what the content of faith is and how the faithful should conduct themselves lose credibility, the Church will stop in its tracks. If Church members lose confidence in their leaders' ability or willingness to speak and live the truth, the Church will be unable to fulfill its purpose.

That, of course, is the worst casualty of these crises of authority. It isn't that the Church will lose members. It isn't that the Church will lose assets. It isn't that the Church will lose prestige. It is that the Church will be disabled, incapable of fulfilling its mission that is, as noted in Chapter Three, "making all things new," transforming society to open the way to salvation. To avoid that outcome and to recapture its teaching and moral authority, the Catholic Church must be willing to embrace a new understanding and exercise of authority.

If a prescription could be written as to how to accomplish this sort of restoration, it would have been published long before this book. Becoming an authoritative force again in the lives of believers and unbelievers is not achieved via a clear and easy path. There is risk involved. There is uncertainty. It will require a certain amount of faith and even more courage. It will mean entering into the cycle of death and resurrection, losing oneself to find oneself. Members of the Church – those who exercise authority and those who respond – will have to examine their experiences of authority to search out its nature and its dynamics. Elements of authority will have to be

Frederick J. Sneesby

identified and analyzed, in far more profound ways than was done at the beginning of this chapter, in order to arrive at an honest and solid foundation for the preaching and action of the Church. How authority is invested in certain roles, how experience refines and expands authority, how authority serves the wider perspective, how authority grows from community and tradition, how authority must serve others' experiences and inspirations, how authority is validated by suffering, how authority supersedes convention, how it guides and prompts people to reach for the ideal and the infinite ... all of these aspects of authority that were described earlier and more will inform the Church as to what it must change to be, once more, the light and leaven of the world.

CHAPTER SIX

ABORTION

Through the last decades of the twentieth century and into the twenty-first, serious struggles have come and gone on the marquee of civic life: farm workers' rights, the Vietnam War, and nuclear disarmament to name a few about which Catholics debated and acted from their faith. The one that has remained for the last four decades, though, is abortion.

There is not a more divisive issue, mostly because both "sides" cling to their positions with such dogmatic certitude. The battle lines are very clear on each anniversary of Roe v. Wade or on the eve of key legislative votes: "pro-life" demonstrators who frighten the general populace by their gruesome campaign and the "pro-choice" counter-demonstrators who astound us by their cold denial of the realities of abortion. The blame for the "pro-life" camp's perceived fanaticism and rigidity is unequivocally placed on religion. "The "anti-choice" crowd only wants to impose their religious beliefs on everyone else," says the "pro-choice" contingent. Intransigence, however, does not require religious belief. Acting like the reproductive wing of the NRA, the pro-abortion faithful will not budge an inch or admit any limit on a person's right to abort a developing fetus. Their positions are equally unbending. The ongoing debate between these two parties is really a faith debate because it has shown no patience for fact or science and great appetite for creedal statements. Belief is belief, religious or not.

For any discussion about abortion to be fruitful, it must be understood that abortion is not a religious issue. It can be examined and debated and decided upon without reference to religion. It is not a religious matter anymore than any other issue is. Civil rights. Foreign policy. Stem cells. Same-sex marriage. Property rights. The Middle East. Taxation. None of these is a religious issue. And they all are. That is the paradox within the relationship between religion and politics. Political, economic, and social realities can be lived and vetted without reference to religion. For believers, however, everything is religious. Their God is at the center of all that is and their faith illuminates every facet of life. No exception. For politicians who are believers, this is a major stumbling block. It is, as well, for the average voter who believes. If that politician or that voter happens to be Catholic, the degree of difficulty is raised a few notches.

The majority of politicians and voters avoid the possible clash between their religion and their politics by making believe. They pretend that it is possible to think about, form opinions, and vote on public policy without reference to their faith. They place their religion in a compartment separate from the affairs of the world as if their faith has nothing to do with politics and economics and the business of everyday life. They invoke the sacred dogma of "separation of church and state" as if that excuses them from examining their political actions with the eyes of faith. They pretend that in the war of convictions, they can be the neutral Switzerland and somehow conduct a public life sanitized from religious influence and devoid of any belief. They are fooling themselves. Every politician and every voter is operating from a set of beliefs, religious or secular.

Abortion continues to be the subject of fierce political and cultural debate because it is one of the most fundamental issues of our time. The issue of abortion is not at the periphery of our cultural and political life. It is not one issue among many. It cuts to the very core of what it means to be a civil society, a moral people, a nation in which everyone has standing no matter her status, ability, possession, or appearance. The resolution of this debate will determine whether or not the value of human life is subject to an individual's whim, whether or not its worth is calculated by how useful it may be or by how much another is invested in it, and whether or not the value of human life is grounded in standards established by human reason. The struggle to extend the protection of the law to unborn human life is not just about individual fetuses, it is also about the dignity and value of all human life, it is about revering human relationships and the obligations that arise from them, it is about insisting that right and wrong are not determined by caprice or power but by reason and law. Much is at stake and so the debate will not go away anytime soon.

American Catholics find themselves in the eye of the abortion storm. Although abortion can be considered apart from religion, American Catholics cannot avoid this as a religious issue. The Catechism of the Catholic Church (Part III, Section Two, Chapter 2, Article 5, Paragraphs 2270-2275) states the teaching of the Church very plainly and strongly, that direct procured abortion is a moral evil "gravely contrary to the moral law." The issue of abortion is putting American Catholics to a severe test of faith and many are failing. Before examining this test of faith further and how the American Church is responding, it is useful to look a little more deeply into why the debate about abortion is so fundamental and crucial to American life.

The "pro-choice" viewpoint maintains that a person should be able to choose to destroy a developing human life up to the point of birth for any reason or for no reason and without any reference to another person or family or larger social unit, or government. It would be hard to find a more highly individualistic tenet. It is very odd that many of the same people who passionately preach that it takes a village to raise a child, also steadfastly maintain that it only takes an individual to destroy one. One can get caught up into the particulars of the abortion debate: when the fetus is viable, the possibility of the fetus feeling pain, the outer time limits of acceptable abortion up through partial birth procedures, the degree to which the woman's rights supersede the fetus' right to life, and on and on, all the specific arguments that are endlessly debated. However, in order to understand fully the significance of the abortion debate in the United States, it is important to go beyond the particular pro-choice positions on abortion and "abortion rights" and examine the presuppositions or first principles of the pro-choice stance. The reasoning and world-view of the pro-choice position are as terrifying and dangerous to society's well-being as the actual destruction of developing human life that takes place in any abortion.

To say that a person may decide to destroy a human fetus solely on his or her own, without any necessary reference to others, presumes several things. First of all, it presumes that no obligation is attached to the most elemental social bond, the relationship of mother and fetus. Can there be a deeper or more fundamental social bond than this relationship? Yet, in the pro-choice view, there is no social obligation arising from this bond. No obligation of care or safeguarding or basic protection. The bond carries with it no debt even at the most primitive level. The womb has become a precarious and dangerous place to be. The fetus can be treated as a stranger or even an enemy.

Does it not follow that if this most fundamental of human connections is disregarded then other human relationships will also be rendered meaningless? If the mother-fetus bond is so fragile and easily dismissed, why would the relationships of neighbor to neighbor, parent to child, spouse to spouse, or citizen to fellow citizen be held any more sacred? Yet, many pro-choice advocates would insist on a series of obligations arising from social ties. For example, in the Prologue to his book, *The Audacity of Hope*, President Barack Obama passionately calls for a renewal of the bonds of social obligation, calling on the American "collective conscience" and "common set of values," "shared language" and "shared understandings." Later in the book, he states that he believes "our communal values, our sense of mutual responsibility and social solidarity" should express themselves in government. One has to wonder how he can presume any sort of social solidarity or mutual obligation in a country in which no one, including the mother, has any obligation to or responsibility for a fetus s/he has brought to life. For one of the most extreme pro-abortion rights national politicians to wax on about "social solidarity" is either dishonest, or unthinking. Remember that the pro-choice position is that a person should be able to choose to destroy a developing human life up to the point of birth for any reason or for no reason and without any reference to another person or family or larger social unit, or government, or principle. Throughout his political career, President Obama advocated for the arbitrary destruction of the most basic social bond; how can he then expect that any sense of social obligation will endure in this country?

If one person can decide life or death without the requirement of consulting with anybody, the bonds of family are also made impotent and meaningless. If a man decides that the child he has created with a woman must be aborted and forces her to seek an abortion, the role of that woman as mother, wife, partner, is nullified. The same would be true if the woman seeks an abortion without consultation with the father. And what about the grandparents, brothers and sisters, and extended family? Everyone gets excluded from this decision and act. No social bond is recognized. As long as it is perfectly legal for an individual to destroy a developing human life without reference to anyone else, the devastating effect on society remains the same: no one else counts beyond the individual.

The nuclear and extended families are not the only social units barred from the decision to abort. Any government interest is also denied. According to the pro-choice position, the government has no interest or role in the fate of developing human life. When you think about the many things government is expected to do in this day and age, and about how many ways the government interferes or intervenes in everyday life, this pro-choice prohibition against government is astonishing. What is not regulated by the state? A person cannot go fishing without going to the government to get a license. Someone cannot put an addition on her house or operate a vehicle without the government somehow interfering with her choices and her freedom. Yet in this most basic and most fundamental of interests, that is, bearing children and bringing human life into existence, the pro-choice position is saying that the government cannot regulate this or intervene in this at all.

If government cannot intervene at all in this most basic matter of the preservation of developing human life, if government has no legitimate interest in this most elemental human relationship of parent and child, how can it claim competence or authority to intervene in other matters? If we say that the state has no interest, no power, and no grounds upon which to regulate or to intervene in this situation, how can we say that the state is justified to intervene in or to regulate other human exchanges or relationships? The presuppositions of the extreme pro-choice stance eat away at the foundations of things like public education, public assistance for the needy, and many of the social programs on which the more vulnerable have come to depend.

The pro-choice stance leaves the decision to destroy a human fetus to the will of individual people. In the matter of life and death, each individual's standards become absolute. There is no reference to any other authority, such as the state, or to reason, or to any objective rule or principle that might be formulated apart from the opinions of individuals. Each person becomes an absolute moral agent whose standards of right and wrong have equal footing with everyone else's. The judgment of the individual is absolute. With each person's being a separate and absolute moral agent with his or her own moral code that may or may not align with others', the country becomes populated with millions of autonomous moral agents with an equal number of moral codes. In such a scenario, it becomes impossible to compare one moral judgment against another or to say that one person's moral code is superior or inferior. There is no common standard, no broader or higher authority to which to appeal or against which a person's moral code may be assessed. Right and wrong cannot be discovered by turning to objective data or reasoning, community values or community authority. Right and wrong become functions of whoever has enough power to impose his or her will on others. Right and wrong, justice and injustice are decided not by the rule of reason but by the person with the most power. Dialogue about moral issues becomes impossible because there is no shared ethical vocabulary or reasoning. Society becomes morally disabled. The weak and the vulnerable lose out in this type of society in which moral reasoning, authority and obligation are reduced to the caprice of the individual. Ultimately, in this kind of society, the powerful dictate right and wrong.

The most pernicious consequence of the pro-choice worldview is that innocent life has no objective value apart from what others invest in it. There used to be a radio talk show host in my listening area who was a prominent pro-abortionist. I tuned in to her show one day and she was doing a show about the grief women feel after a miscarriage. Given her strong support for absolute abortion rights, I really did think she was joking by hosting such a show. But she wasn't! A horrifying realization came over me that this woman regarded the fetus as a person if the mother grieved for it after a miscarriage but believed that the fetus was not a person if the mother simply wanted the fetus dead through abortion. If the fetus cannot appeal to science or reason to gain some intrinsic value that exists beyond the feelings or designs of individuals, can any other vulnerable member of our society such as the homeless, the undocumented, or the disabled hope to hold onto some social standing that rests on reason and the rule of law and not the whim of an individual?

What our culture is left with is a bleak individualism that says to the unborn and to all who do not have power, "You are on your own." Can there be a worldview that is more destructive than this? Can there be a set of beliefs that is more antithetical to Catholic belief than this? Yet there are many Catholic politicians, local and national, who espouse the pro-choice position. There are millions more Catholic voters who do the same. At the same time, the position that developing human life deserves the protection of the law is central to Catholic moral teaching. It is not a minor issue. It is not one that allows for a wide spectrum of opinion. It, in fact, springs from a fundamental belief in the sacredness of human life, even in the womb.

One can debate the abortion issue without reference to religion. But if a politician professes to be Catholic, he or she really cannot pretend that his or her opinions and votes about abortion can be decided without reference to his or her faith, nor can the average voter. I know that many Catholics do, making a peculiar distinction between their "personal" beliefs and their public stances as if they can believe in two separate and irreconcilable truths. There are many prominent Catholics who are perfectly comfortable with this pretense.

Is the Catholic Church in the United States fiercely and unequivocally defending the value of human life starting in the womb? Sadly, the answer is, no. Although there are many local right-to-life groups, lawyers who argue cases, legislators who sponsor bills, ordinary people who cling to a belief in the sanctity of human life, and others who are fighting the tide of extreme individualism and materialism that is at the heart of the pro-abortion movement, the Catholic Church is divided in the pews and in the pulpits. Only a tiny minority would claim to be "pro-choice Catholics" but a large number of Catholics who accept the label "pro-life" – laity, clergy, and religious – remain silent, invoking the virtue of tolerance in a pluralistic society. Catholic leadership is giving very mixed signals to Catholics and non-Catholics because what they say and what they do don't match.

There are really two issues here. One is the prevalence among Catholics of the faulty reasoning that comes to the conclusion that "While I am opposed to abortion on demand, I cannot impose my beliefs on others." "We cannot legislate morality" is another version of this way of thinking. The other issue is the Church's reluctance to oppose mainstream culture and political power publicly.

"I believe personally that abortion is morally wrong but I believe that the decision to terminate a pregnancy is a matter between a woman and her doctor, therefore, I support a woman's right to choose." This statement has been confessed by Catholic politicians many times since Roe v. Wade and seconded by Catholic voters. One or another version of this thought has been trafficked for a few decades even though it is one of the most questionable assertions imaginable.

The taking of human life is an evil. Can we all agree on this? There may be instances when causing this evil is justified. Can we all agree on this? The most commonly accepted instances would be killing an attacker in self-defense (unless some less drastic measure would stop the attack) and killing an enemy in a just war (sort of the self-defense case on the scale of nations). Until the latter part of the twentieth century, very few have argued that the taking of innocent and defenseless human life can be justified.

It is at this point that the "I believe personally that abortion is wrong but ..." argument becomes difficult to follow because the next deduction is that this judgment, that the taking of human life is evil, should not be inscribed in law. Rather, individuals should be able to make that decision and take that step unencumbered by any communal, political, or legal consideration. This leap in reasoning leaves some behind. In other words, those who think that this instance of taking human life is an evil also think it should be perfectly legal. It is incongruent to the point of absurdity. It is almost as absurd as thinking that there is a wall between the law and morality; that somehow all the laws that exist in the nation remain untainted by any brand of morality. But many people hold these views.

How has it come about that a sizable percentage of Catholics – and the percentage is still surprisingly high even when polling Catholics who attend church regularly – is perfectly at ease espousing beliefs that are completely at odds with Church teaching on one of the most fundamental of moral issues? Even more remarkable is the comfort level of Catholic politicians who do the same but more prominently as they spread a new Gospel with their public statements and create new moral boundaries by what they vote into law.

In my home state, there is a sitting United States senator who is Catholic and Irish-American. A few years ago, the local chapter of the Friendly Sons of St. Patrick honored him as "Man of the Year" at their annual St. Patrick's Day dinner. I'm sure St. Patrick smiled down on their gathering as they give this award to a politician who is a champion of abortion on demand, even partial-birth abortion. I don't know how far back in the senator's ancestry were the actual immigrants (maybe it was his grandparents or great-grandparents) but you can bet they did not espouse this most extreme position. My questions are, how did we get from the Great-Grandfather to the Senator and what happened to the values in-between? The senator may protest that he personally is against abortion but that, because he must represent all citizens, he cannot impose his own beliefs on others. The presumption is that the values of his heritage must give way to those of the generic American culture. Somehow, because they carry the label "religious," these beliefs also become idiosyncratic; thus, they are pushed out of the public arena, disqualified from the public debate, stripped of the legitimacy granted secular beliefs, quarantined.

It could be asked, when may a person's or a group's beliefs be imposed on others through a lawful process? After all, beliefs are imposed all the time by legislatures and courts. When may a person's or a group's values, whether their origins be religious or not, apply also to the rest of society? When may some one or some group expect that the rest of society accept and even adopt its beliefs? Values that are based in beliefs peculiar to a certain group (and such a group may have a religious, cultural, or purely civic or humanitarian identity) will disappear in the confrontation with the general culture unless they find a basis beyond the purely sectarian. For example, the insistence that human life deserves the protection of the law at all stages may be inspired by the Scriptures or by the teachings of various churches or by the principles of a sub-culture, but unless it also finds a basis in human reason it can never make intellectual and moral demands on all of the population. The group's value must find a footing beyond the group. The main "crossing over" point is human reason. The truth of the matter is that everyone who has anything to say about abortion in the public arena is speaking from some belief even if he or she is an atheist or agnostic. There is no belief-neutral stance. Everyone is operating from beliefs, values, and first principles religious or non-religious. So religious people should never apologize for their beliefs or let themselves be disqualified because they are believers

The main question of this chapter, though, is how can it be that the public stance of many Catholics on the fundamental issue of abortion is indistinguishable from that of mainstream American culture? It appears that nothing will be fiercely maintained by American Catholics if it would too strongly distinguish them from the rest of society. The American Catholic Church has become more American than Catholic. Faithfulness to the Gospel, devotion to the truth, and the anchoring of human life in the life of the divine have been pushed aside for social legitimacy, cultural homogenization, and a vacuous tolerance that masquerades as intellectual or civic maturity.

The Catholic hierarchy has not helped matters. They long ago made the teaching authority of the Church hollow by their insistence on condemning artificial birth control. Years later, their moral authority crumbled with every new revelation of clergy sexual abuse and the accompanying complicity or incompetence of

Church leaders. Is it any wonder, then, that the foundational moral teaching protecting unborn human life and prohibiting abortion would, astonishingly, carry no particular weight with vast numbers of American Catholics? That seems to be the case, though. It is apparent that the teaching Church has failed to communicate even the most basic moral reasoning and truths to Catholics. How else would you explain that so many Catholics claim that while they believe abortion in most instances is wrong and immoral, they don't want to force their views on anyone and so the decision to abort should be left up to the individual?

The failure of the teaching authority of the Church on abortion is compounded with each instance of seeming appeasement or cowardice on the part of the Catholic hierarchy. In 2008, at a crucial point of the presidential campaign, a photo of the Cardinal of New York at the annual Al Smith Charity Dinner yukking it up with Barack Obama, one of the most extreme pro-abortion politicians of the day, was plastered across every media outlet in the nation. A picture is worth a thousand words, and those words began, "It is OK to hold abortion views such as his …." The same scandalous Al Smith Charity Dinner mistake was made just before the 2012 presidential campaign. And in 2009, the now President Obama was invited to speak at the commencement of Notre Dame University, the premier Catholic university in many Americans' minds. With Notre Dame's invitation, every Catholic in the U.S. was confronted with a tacit endorsement of an extreme pro-abortion stance. "We like the way he thinks" was the message communicated.

As a nation we need to decide at which point human life deserves the protection of the law. Catholics need to be forcing this decision, insisting on the absolute value of human life and the status of developing human life in our society. Certainly, no Catholic politician who is unreservedly pro-choice from either political party should go unchallenged. Further, no pro-choice politician should go unchallenged regardless of his or her religious brand. Bishops or any Catholic person who addresses issues such as abortion should be addressing their remarks to two different audiences: Catholics (including the Catholic politician) and non-Catholics. Many public Church pronouncements are crafted this way; when they are meant for a wider audience than Church members, they usually begin with words like, "to my brothers and sisters in Christ and to all people of good will." Bishops' statements about abortion should follow a similar method; they should speak to the baptized Catholic but also to everyone else who is touched by the issue.

Catholic politicians need to be directly counseled by their bishops and other pastoral leaders that they are in serious violation of Catholic moral teaching. Other Catholics need to be alerted to the fact that these politicians are clearly at odds with what it means to be a Catholic. Catholic teachers have a responsibility, indeed a duty, to do this. Catholic teaching authorities should speak to them and about them (to other Catholics) using the language of the Catholic faith and culture. Certainly, it is scandalous that a professed Catholic should be trumpeting a position so diametrically opposed to one of the most fundamental of Church moral teachings. Beyond scandalous, it is embarrassing. How could a Catholic be raised and educated in the Faith and end up with a pro-choice position?

But what about everyone else? What are Catholic bishops and teachers supposed to be saying to non-Catholic Americans? Should they be saying anything at all? Because the practice of abortion is one of the most fundamental matters of this or any era, Catholic and other religious leaders should be speaking out as loudly as possible to non-believers about abortion. They must fight in the public arena with reason and data and all manner of persuasion that is accessible to everyone, not just the religious believer. For Catholics, this is an almost natural thing to do. Catholics believe in the compatibility of faith and reason. As a Catholic, I was taught never to fear the truth because it would never contradict my faith. Catholics should be fighting this fight to give the unborn the protection of the law by

Frederick J. Sneesby

engaging every person of good will in pursuit of the truth about the practice of abortion in a way that makes sense to him or her.

If American Catholics cannot stand for this most basic good, does being a Catholic in America have any meaning at all?

CHAPTER SEVEN

USUAL SUSPECTS

I n news stories and in everyday conversations about the Catholic Church, there are "usual suspects," that is, topics on which people always focus. A lot of it centers on the priesthood: women priests, married priests, and priest abusing children. Other conversations will drift into the political sphere, something upon which we have already touched. Here we will look at women in the Catholic Church, married priests, and clergy abusing children.

Women

My daughters cannot become Catholic priests. Let's just start there. There is no way to know if God would ever call them to the priesthood. If they were to hear that call and could answer it, they would be excellent priests. As it is, they are prevented from responding to a vocation to the priesthood. Maybe that's all that has to be said about women and the Catholic Church: our daughters are barred from the priesthood because of their gender.

Back in the early 1980's, I would visit the parish school and recruit altar boys from the 6th grade. Without fail, the girls would raise their hands and ask if they could be altar servers. (In those days, girls were not allowed to be altar servers.) I would give the same response each year. I would say, no, and then write the name and address of the bishop on the board and recommend that they write to him and ask to be altar servers. They would. And, to his credit, he would write back. He would also say, no, and his reasoning went along the lines of all the apostles being men and so we know that Jesus intended priests to be men as well, and altar servers are "acolytes" and acolyte used to be one of the "Minor Orders" that led to priesthood, and so on. Even the 6th grade girls knew that didn't make much sense. Female altar servers are now commonplace as are female lectors, extraordinary ministers of communion, catechists, and parish administrators to name just a few of the roles filled by women in the Catholic Church. There is a very definite line in the sand, though, drawn around Holy Orders – no female priests, no female deacons.

Besides the gap between First and Third World Catholics and the clergy abuse of children, there cannot be a greater scandal in the Catholic Church than the exclusion of women from ordination. It is wrong. It is sinful. There's no getting around it.

Most of the arguments for an all-male clergy begin by depending heavily on a narrow Christo-centric theology – that the priest is "another Christ" or "alter Christus" as it is usually expressed as if saying it in Latin makes it less questionable – and end up de-valuing women. Catholic women are, of course, other Christs because they are baptized. Broader and deeper explanations of roles and offices in the Church employ language centered on the action of the Holy Spirit, explanations that do not find gender a stumbling block. The arguments for ordaining women are, in my opinion, more reasonable than those for an all-male clergy and have a basis in Scripture and the tradition of the early Church. There are excellent books to which you can refer about ordaining women priests. The topic is raised here because excluding women from ordination is a major obstacle to the Church's fulfilling its mission.

It is a hard issue to unpack because the theology and doctrine are so bound up with gender politics, sexual biases, and cultures. In fact, theology and religious talk really get in the way of discovering what the real issues are at stake in the "women priests" debate. In my estimation, the main reason that women are not priests is power. The unmarried men who run the Church do not want to give up control, so they employ their ecclesiastical authority and marshal any theological argument they can grab in a storm and they hold fast. I do not judge their motivation. They may be resisting this change for what they believe are good reasons, but they are clinging to their power nonetheless. In doing so, they are weakening the Church's ability to accomplish what it is supposed to be doing.

How can the Church preach and teach credibly on any subject if it holds such an indefensible position? More particularly, how can the Church address what have been popularly designated as "women's rights" issues if they offend women by barring them from the priestly office? How can the Church defend women in countries where they are excluded from formal education, made servants of men, and disqualified from fundamental human rights if the Church itself is oppressing women? The Church's treatment of women is robbing the Church of its voice on crucial matters.

John 8:1-11 is the passage about the authorities bringing the woman caught in adultery to Jesus to demand his opinion, an opinion they were hoping would set him at odds with cultural and religious authority. They knew very well that the accepted penalty for a woman caught in adultery was to stone her to death. You probably know the story. They got their wish; Jesus did respond. He took his time, though, taking some of the wind out of the self-righteous' sails by bending down and writing absent-mindedly in the dirt. It doesn't say what he wrote – I would love to know. Not to be sacrilegious, but it must have been something bordering on an expletive directed at that crowd. Anyway, he eventually straightened up and made one withering suggestion, "Let him who is without sin cast the first stone."

No stones came flying (Yes, I do remember the old joke about one stone landing near Jesus' feet and his saying, "Mom, I didn't mean you."). In fact, everyone left and the woman was freed for a life of goodness by her conversation with Jesus.

Upon hearing this story, doesn't it occur to you immediately that they are still stoning women for adultery in different parts of the world? In some more enlightened countries, they don't stone them; they only lash them brutally with canes. This story in the Gospel of John is, first and foremost, an example and message of forgiveness that has been welcomed and celebrated in the centuries since the stones remained on the ground in that public square. But more to our point, the story is about equality. It was apparent to the crowd threatening the woman and has been clear to all those who subsequently have heard this story, that Jesus, with his invitation to the sinless to throw the first stone, was putting everyone on the same footing. He was very plainly saying that this woman and everyone else are equal. Unlike his word of forgiveness, however, this message of equality has not been welcomed and celebrated since that day. Women are still being stoned, women are still being brutally oppressed, and women are still seen as not equal to men. Most of us are complicit in this sin against women.

In the scene with Jesus and the hostile crowd, who were the guilty ones? It wasn't just the people with stones in their hands. It was all the onlookers, all those who never questioned the adultery laws, and all those who held power by taking it away from women. In the present day, there is similar guilt to go around. Yes, we can shake our heads in disbelief that there are still societies in which women are punished by stoning. We can raise our eyebrows in amazement that large portions of the world population do not allow women to go to school or to function freely; women are forced to wear restrictive clothing and to do men's bidding. But we should not fool ourselves; the threads of guilt for the oppression of women lead to our own society. There are many things about us that put stones in our hands.

The swimsuit edition of *Sports Illustrated* is there for all, even my young daughters, to see at the grocery checkouts. Trumping the news of genocide in Africa and crisis in the Middle East is the news of various female celebrities exposing themselves. Beauty queens are named and then censured for stepping outside norms. The cutting edge of consumer technology has been, in modern times, the pornography industry. The worries of women are not government and business and culture, but clothing and makeup and shopping. The distribution of domestic work in far too many families is still weighted toward the women. In whatever way we are part of the trivializing of women, we are at least in the crowd of onlookers. Besides these individual examples of oppression, we can turn our eyes to what our governments, businesses, boards of directors, managers, corporate offices, civic institutions, etc. look like when viewed through the eyeglass of gender. How are we changing things so that women are there?

Let's not forget the churches. The oppression of women is one of the great sins of the Catholic Church. We are not stoning them, but we are aiding all those who persecute women by discriminating against them in our Church. Who is pressing the fight for equal participation of women in the life of the Church? For the Church to be effective, women must be admitted to the priesthood.

Married Priests

There's nothing intrinsically wrong with unmarried men. They can be good priests. So can married men. And women. Married and unmarried. All of these can live and preach the Gospel and celebrate the sacraments.

There are, of course, married men who are functioning as Roman Catholic priests. Some years ago, the way was cleared so that Episcopalian priests who became Catholic could then be ordained as Catholic priests. I remember when the first one of these was ordained a priest in the Diocese of Providence where I was serving as a priest. He was married, a father, and a grandfather. At the time, I belonged to a small group of priests called "Priests for Justice" who spoke out about various issues and who gave unsolicited advice to the bishop. Right after the married Episcopalian was ordained, we held a regular meeting. The subject of the ordination came up and one of the members of the group was uncharacteristically angry and even bitter at this development. It wasn't long after that he left the priesthood and married. At the time I thought to myself how offensive ordaining a married man must have been to him who was, obviously, struggling with celibacy.

Of course, there are many who struggle with celibacy and who remain priests and celibate. If their celibacy is linked with a life of simplicity that leads to a generous ministry, these celibates give valuable witness to the realities that are beyond this world. If, however, their lives become skewed in some way – towards excess or clericalism or resentment – then they give witness to an inexcusable cruelty that is visited upon those who take on celibacy as the price of ministry.

Allowing married men to be priests, or women, married or unmarried, to be ordained, will change the priesthood. This change will, in turn, demand major adjustments by the laity and more of their talent and pocketbook.

The priest's job description would change. He or she will do less, which means that others in the Church would have to do more. For a few decades, now, many more roles have arisen in the Church – most of them being dusted off from earlier centuries – and the work of the Church has been done by many more and different people. Liturgically, it is seen in the ministries of lector and Eucharistic minister. There are directors of religious education and finance councils and ministers of music. There are people ministering in prisons and hospitals and many other places fulfilling many other functions. Considering this expansion of ministry in the Church, one could say that there is no vocation shortage but rather a vocation boom. In my own biased view, the diminished numbers of vocations to the priesthood and the growing numbers of vocations to other ministries in the Church demonstrate that God is pushing and pulling the Church away from a dominant priesthood and toward a different way of doing things.

It must be remembered that the inclusion of women and married people in the priesthood will not, by itself, change the way ministry is done or the way power and authority are exercised within the Church or bridge the separation between clergy and laity. In fact, if women and married people were ordained tomorrow, there would be plenty of priests and the Church might miss the opportunity to leave clericalism behind and embrace a wider sharing of mission and authority. Perhaps the day when women and married people will be ordained priests will not come until the concentration of power and function in the priesthood is broken down due to lack of priests, and the variety of ministries and ministers needed to fulfill the Church's mission has been firmly established. Certainly, though, having male and female priests, married and unmarried, will soften the distinction between clergy and laity, and that is a necessary ingredient of the more fundamental changes that must take place to insure that the mission of the Church does not get bottled up in clergy-dominated structures.

While the function and power of the priesthood would be more widely shared, the essential identity of the priesthood would be pretty much the same. The priest is a bridge between the divine and the human. He or she dares to keep his eyes open to both worlds and to believe that one is rooted in the other. In this way, he becomes a desperately needed sign of hope. The priest is also learned and, at some point, wise. He is steeped in the Scripture and the Tradition of the Church and acts as teacher and guide. The priest dares to call the faithful to prayer, to pray on their behalf and to preach the Gospel in season and out. By his ministry and example, he unites the lives of the parishioners to the self-sacrifice of Jesus. This is no ordinary calling, to be sure, but let's allow ordinary people to follow it and avoid creating a distinct species or an isolated fraternity of priests.

The selection and training of priests would be just as rigorous as ever, but the pool of candidates would greatly expand.

Clergy Abusing Children

Daniel and Philip Berrigan were brothers who were both ordained priests. They were active leaders in the anti-war movement during the Vietnam War, arrested for breaking into a Selective Service office and pouring blood on the files. I think it was one of the Berrigans who said, "Celibacy gives you the freedom to go to jail." He meant, of course, being completely unencumbered by family concerns to speak against injustice and war even if it included civil disobedience leading to a prison sentence. Serving time for sexually abusing a youngster was not what they had in mind in the days when priests were speaking out for what they thought was right.

Come to think of it though, the priests who preached and picketed against our involvement in Vietnam, who leafleted in support of the Farm Workers union, who protested our support of repressive regimes in Latin America, and who condemned the build-up of nuclear weapons in the early '80's were generally disapproved of. Certainly, they did not hear the degree of condemnation that pedophile priests hear, but they were told to shut up and to stick to spiritual matters and keep religion separate from business and politics and the affairs of the world.

Catholic laity seem to prefer priests who are separated from ordinary life, who are unsullied by the things that most occupy the rest of humanity. They prefer priests who are different, peculiar. They want unmarried men who live, more than likely, alone, in an institutional setting, who don't earn a living wage, who are available 24/7, and who act out a very prescribed role in public settings. They want unmarried men who will be "holy," that is, "other than the rest of us." One suspects that if the laity are successful in somehow "corralling" holiness into a professional class of religious people, then they might just be successful in keeping the real demands of religion away from their everyday lives. Having a distinct class of professional religious people certainly takes the heat off the rest of us when it comes to living the religious life. It may sound harsh to say, and it is somewhat over-stated, but an unmarried, male clergy works very well for laity who would rather be left alone when it comes to the higher mandates of the Gospel.

I remember years ago when the first class of married deacons was ordained in Rhode Island. Many thought it was a great idea. "They'll be a big help to the priests," it was said. But when they started actually getting up to preach on Sundays, the reaction was swift. "Who does he think he is?" "I know his wife and kids." "He teaches my children in school!" "He runs an insurance agency." "Where does he get off getting up there and preaching to us?" The point was that a regular guy had no business acting as a priest would act. Many simply did not want someone up there who was just like the rest of them.

Clearly, this sort of expectation about Catholic clergy has its roots in a tension that exists in Christian religion. God is both transcendent and among us. He is completely "Other" but at the same time one with us. He is total Mystery but also Incarnate. Of course, as fearsome and as awe-inspiring as a faraway God may be, he is most threatening when he is closest because then he might call upon us to change our hearts and our world. Better to keep him at arm's length. Isolating any "high-powered" practice of religion in a separate clerical caste is one very effective way of accomplishing just that.

The outrage expressed at the unlawful sexual practices of some priests is real. But the shock expressed at the behavior of the institutional Church in the face of these awful revelations rings hollow. These things were kept hushed? Civil authorities were not notified? The clergy were intent on taking care of their own? Shocking. But what did the laity expect? They have lived comfortably in a Church where the inner workings of the spiritual life and the real business of religion have been happily handed over to a separate class of people. They have been glad to relinquish responsibility for holiness to a specialized group. A whole sub-culture of the hierarchy and clergy has been created that is removed from the real world and immune to normal scrutiny. But this state of affairs is what Catholic laity have wanted. For psychological, sociological, but mainly spiritual reasons, the laity have handed over the keys to the kingdom to the priests. Having a male, celibate priesthood works for the clergy and the hierarchy to be sure, but more significantly, it works for the laity as well.

Sadly, the whole Church, clergy and laity both are now reaping what they sowed. The awful scandal of hundreds of priests abusing thousands of children reveals a fundamental difficulty in the Church: a spiritual apartheid that separates clergy and laity, a deification of the priesthood that may lead to unhealthy lives, and an "aristocratization" of the clergy that leaves power and control in the hands of the ordained. Much has been sacrificed to maintain the political status quo in the Catholic Church. In doing so, we are failing the One who entrusted a mission to us at the very beginning. The message is being compromised and the saving grace of a confident community of faith is being lost. We really need a vibrant Church these days. People need to know why they are here. Peace needs to be insisted upon even in the deafening sounds of war. The poor and the vulnerable need a champion. The rich and the comfortable need to be challenged. Life in all its forms needs to be defended. Sacrificial love needs to be preached and lived. But the Church is not fulfilling these needs. The creation and acceptance of a peculiar priesthood has provided a breeding ground for aberrant behavior, and the consequent clergy abuse scandal has desiccated the Church's preaching vitality.

CHAPTER EIGHT

EMBRACING AND REJECTING A MEDIOCRE CHURCH

*A*madeus won the Academy Award for the Best Picture of the Year in 1984. I didn't see it until several years later but very quickly became captivated by this film. In the movie, Antonio Salieri, a respected court composer in Vienna in the eighteenth century, becomes obsessed with Wolfgang Amadeus Mozart. He immediately recognizes that Mozart is a genius whose music was the "very voice of God." But when he sees that Mozart is such a "giggling, dirty-minded creature" who chases women, drinks too much, has a filthy mouth, and hangs around with the Vienna low life, he becomes tortured by the incongruity and the injustice of such a crude man being blessed by this rare gift of producing divine music. He wonders over and over again why God would choose such a person to be his instrument.

At the end of the movie, Salieri, after attempting suicide, suffers from the delusion that he killed Mozart. He is cared for in an insane asylum and the final scene has him being wheeled through the ward, blessing the other inmates and proclaiming himself the "patron saint of mediocrity … the champion… of mediocrities everywhere."

There are not many Mozarts in the world. There are a lot of Salieri's.

I know that there are over one billion Roman Catholics in the world. The other mainstream Christian Churches are not that big, but they number in the millions. And the major non-Christian organized religions? A lot of people. How many Mozarts among them? I don't mean musical geniuses I mean geniuses of a religious kind. Spiritual prodigies? How many saints? How many zealots? How many martyrs-in-waiting? How many who have left mediocrity behind and have consciously begun to walk down the path of perfection? Only God knows, but I would bet that they are a distinct minority.

The Church is mediocre. The mediocrity started to creep in just after Peter gave his Pentecost address as retold in the Acts of the Apostles and the number of disciples began to inch past the 500 mark. I'm not sure when the mediocrity will disappear; probably just before the Second Coming. This increase in mediocrity should be no surprise to anyone who has been part of a movement or association. Once you get past the founding members, the level of understanding of what the group is all about begins to lower. The degree of dedication to the principles of the group, or the commitment to the group's lifestyle falls off. The message gets watered down. People settle for less. Lenin noted this happening in his revolutionary cells. The more people brought into a group, the more the identity of the group dissipates. It's common sense that this would happen to the Church. It's just disappointing. The Church will fail to meet expectations, whether they are yours or those arising from the Church's own teaching or Jesus'.

If you don't have many expectations, there is no problem here. If you just want to have your children baptized, go through the "growing up" sacraments of First Communion and Confirmation, celebrate marriages and funerals in pleasant Church services and otherwise be left alone, the level of mediocrity in the Church will not bother you. If, however, you think that the Church should be a means of salvation, if you think that the Church has been commissioned by Jesus to bring his message of eternal life to the world, if you think that the Church should be confronting the real evils in the world and fighting to the finish, then the mediocrity of the Church is a constant source of wonderment, frustration, and anger.

The pain of a mediocre Church to the serious believer echoes the pain expressed by St. Paul in three very personal and anguished chapters of his Letter to the Romans. In chapters nine through eleven Paul reveals his sense of loss, confusion, and heartache that his own people, the Jews, whom he loved, did not, as a people, believe in Jesus. It is completely beyond his understanding that the chosen people who had the patriarchs, the covenant, the law, and the prophets, would not accept Jesus as the Messiah.

The Roman Catholic Church could not have a greater heritage. Born from the preaching of the apostles, grown from the seeds of martyrdom, origin and keeper of several civilizations, home to mystics and saints, blessed with the richest theology, graced by the most diverse prayer life, always the hope of the poor and infirm, present in every nation on earth, the Catholic Church holds the greatest promise and possibility. It is not unreasonable to have high expectations of the Church or to be pained, in a way similar to St. Paul, by the Church not living up to its promise.

For those who know Church history, though, the shortcomings of the Church are very familiar. Time and time again, it has sabotaged its own mission, caused pain and suffering, sinned against Scripture and Tradition, ignored the gap between the rich and poor, and favored the powerful over the oppressed. The optimists would say that for every step backwards, the Church has taken two steps forward. They may have a good argument. Looking back over the last 2,000 years, one could easily demonstrate that progress has been made in the world, that God's Kingdom has been realized to a greater degree as the centuries have passed. If the progress is glacial, it is still progress.

In this view, the mediocrity of the Church is less scandalous. The mediocrity of today is the excellence of yesterday. In other words, if one were to compare the state of the Church and of the World today with that of a few centuries ago, we are ahead of the game. We are inching forward. We are accomplishing God's will. At the same time the Church is failing, it is also succeeding, if that makes any sense.

The Church as a whole will never be revolutionary. The clergy and the hierarchy will not make radical changes. The laity will never move rapidly as a body. The Church is not built to be like that. The function of the organizational Church is to maintain a common denominator of belief, prayer, and practice while, almost imperceptibly, raising the bar, increasing the standards that everyone meets.

Revolutionary change comes from other sources within the Church. The bureaucracy will not radically challenge anyone. The usual organizations of parishes and dioceses will not push the faithful to the limit and beyond. It will be the prophets, the mystics, the martyrs, the saints, and the temporary movements within the Church who will cause the Church and the World to reach new heights of holiness and to fulfill its mission of "making all things new" in the world.

Let's look at a few examples. Back in the 1960s through the early 1980s, the Pentecostal Movement in the Catholic Church was expanding and making headlines. Taking its cue from St. Paul's description of the "charismatic" Church of the early days when the gifts ("charisms" from the Greek word for "gift") of the Holy Spirit were evident and prominent in the life and organization of the Church, the Pentecostal or Charismatic Movement prayed for and promoted the exhibition of such gifts in today's Church. Groups blossomed all around the United States on college campuses and in most every parish. In my own diocese, two parishes became (and remain to this day) "charismatic" parishes. Prayer meetings were held and people read the Scriptures and prayed out loud in groups. They encouraged the gifts of speaking in tongues, interpreting the tongues, prophecy, and healing. It was pretty wild stuff for the Catholic Church.

The movement has simmered down in recent years. While it has its pockets of strength – places and leaders who are still very much identified with that approach to spirituality and Church – the movement reached its apogee somewhere in the late '70s and will, more than likely, disappear as a recognizable movement. It leaves behind, though, some lasting benefits. Although the Charismatic Movement was at heart profoundly traditional in spite of its unconventional practices, and, in my opinion, could even be characterized as a reactionary movement, it pushed the Church forward in some significant areas. Because of the Charismatic Movement and others contemporary with it like the Cursillo Movement and the Christian Family Movement, three things took hold in the Church and are now an accepted part of Church life: lay leadership, open prayer in groups, and devotion to the study and reading of the Scripture.

These are examples of temporary movements pushing the Church forward, causing change at a much faster pace than what would normally be generated by the usual structures within the Church. Individuals can also be agents of change, people who might fit the descriptions of mystics or saints and who have brought new life and expanded horizons to the Church: Pope John XXIII, Thomas Merton, and Mother Teresa among others.

The Church, therefore, in its widest presentation, can be quite revolutionary. Don't expect the normal structures and leaders of the Church to be that, though. They have other functions to fulfill. What are we to do then in the face of this maddeningly enormous and slow-to-move group of one billion people whose leaders are hesitant and whose everyday life doesn't seem to be on the cutting edge of God's Kingdom? Is it even fair to hold the Catholic Church in the United States, or any country, to the standard of martyrdom?

When St. Paul was grappling with the problem of the Jews rejecting Jesus in those chapters in Romans, he recalled how Elijah railed against Israel in his time because they had abandoned God. God reminded Elijah that there was a small group within Israel who was still faithful. Paul translates that to his own time and writes, "Just so, in the present time there is a remnant chosen by the grace of God." Paul is convinced that no matter how small this remnant may be, or no matter how far things have drifted from the way they ought to be, God will turn things around because, His "gifts and His call are irrevocable." He ends these chapters with hope, writing that once the "full number of Gentiles enter in, then all Israel will be saved," and faith, exclaiming "How inscrutable His judgments, how unsearchable His ways," believing in God's power to bring about the good even though Paul himself does not see how that will happen. For those who come to the point of despair with the Church, these are valuable lessons: recognizing that the revolutionary and the reactionary forces within the Church move the whole Church forward in their pushing and pulling, hoping that the irrevocability of God's promise to the Church will bring about what He intends, and believing that the Holy Spirit is at work although it is sometimes difficult to make that act of faith.

It would be a great loss to give up on the promise of the Church. There is a tremendous temptation, especially in the United States with its deep culture of individualism, to abandon the notion of church and organized religion and to strike out on one's own in the religious life. Increasingly, people view membership in a church as an obstacle to authentic spiritual life. That, in my mind, is a serious mistake. Rather than argue that the Church is a liability and burden to Jesus' mission, I would insist on the inevitability and necessity of the Church. A relationship with Jesus includes a relationship with a church, that is, with others.

For illustration, consider an elemental human relationship, marriage. Don't let anyone tell you that you only marry an individual. You always, always marry that person's family, for better and for worse. My background is Anglo. One grandmother came from Ireland and a grandfather came from England. Even though there were seven children in my family, whenever we were at the dinner table, only one person spoke at a time and the others listened. I guess it was sort of an echo of the English "queuing up" to get on the bus. You can imagine my culture shock, therefore, the first time I went for dinner at the family of my future wife, whose four grandparents were from Italy. Everyone talked at once. There were several conversations going on at the same time. Those who waited withered. And the verbal free for all could also get a little heated, with the decibel level getting to a point that in my family signaled a declaration of war. It was like *Sense and Sensibility* meets *My Cousin Vinny* (I remember watching *Sense and Sensibility* with my wife and turning to her as the credits rolled and remarking, "If that family had been Italian, the movie would have been over in five minutes because someone would have grabbed the guy and demanded, "Are you going to marry my sister or not?")

By marriage, I am now Italian. When I married my wife, I didn't just get Sandy. I got her parents and brothers, her aunts, uncles and cousins. The food and the customs. The passion and the loyalty. The vocabulary and the immigrant history. I got it all even though I only married one person. You can't just marry an individual. You always marry that person's family members either in person or their ghosts. In the same way, I would maintain that no one can believe in Jesus or have any sort of relationship with him without having a relationship with a church. If anyone thinks that he or she can love and follow Jesus and not belong to a church, he is fooling himself. It cannot be done. This is a crucial point in understanding one's spiritual life. If you want Jesus, there has to be a church. No church, no Jesus.

Certainly it is so much neater and more pleasant just to deal with Jesus. Read about him in the Scriptures. Think about him. Try to imitate him. Pray to him. Just accomplishing these things is a pretty tall order. If someone did all of this, he would consider himself a religious success. Unfortunately, his religious journey would be incomplete without a church.

Not to be Clintonesque, but what do we mean by "church"? Is it the Gothic cathedral with incense hanging heavy in the air and grim-looking clergy lurking in the shadows? Maybe. Is it the steel and glass inter- and/or non- denominational Christian church that has its own gymnasium and investment club? Maybe. Is it the storefront First Church of the Apostles of Christ the Good Shepherd that meets every night of the week? Maybe. Is it just you and your wife and kids trying to remember to say Grace before eating? Maybe. Is it you and the guy in the next cubicle at work who share horror stories of growing up in Catholic school while doing volunteer work at the local Food Bank? Maybe. Does that mean that any sort of group can be a church? Maybe. Maybe not. There are certain characteristics that a group must possess in order to be a "church."

If a group is to think of itself as a Christian church, it must be a church of Jesus. No matter how many people may belong to the "church," two, three, thousands, or millions, no group can be a Christian church unless they are brought together by Jesus. He is the reason they gather. He gives meaning to what they do together. He challenges them to grow and heals them when they are broken. There may be other bonds - blood, marriage, nationality, profession, class, race, interest – but the shared relationship with Jesus is what makes the group more than it would be, it makes the group a church.

The group that would be a church is marked by choice. The call of Jesus has to be accepted by the members of the group and mutually acknowledged. In other words, belonging to a church has to be a conscious act and a consciousness that is shared. It's not enough to inherit church membership or go to Sunday service week after week on automatic pilot. It's not enough to sit in the pew avoiding eye contact with other churchgoers.

To be a church, the group has to pray together. That's brilliant. Of course they have to pray together! But it's important to mention this fact because "churches" end up doing so many other things. The fundraisers, the social events, the committees, religious education, Christmas toy drives, manning the soup kitchen, and on and on. Prayer. Together.

The life of the group must be marked by service. I used to love those two guys in the peanut gallery in *The Muppets* sitting on the sidelines and making comments, and "Sam the Eagle" would pronounce judgment on everyone else. They were funny. But that's not what the Church is supposed to do. The Church cannot be some righteous blowhard who judges and condemns and is satisfied to let the world go to ruin as long as the chosen few are saved. No, the Church must serve the rest of the world, especially the poor and especially sinners. The Church must wash the feet of the world.

To be a church, the group must experience ever-expanding relationships. The Spirit of Jesus leads you beyond yourself to form a community with at least one other person, and then it leads that community beyond itself to embrace others who would not otherwise be part of that community. The bonds of a real Church are not based on blood or race or nationality or shared interests or economic class. The bond is the Spirit of Love that forms unnatural communities. In this way, a Church is very different from a club or association. The test of a real Church is not just the shared relationship with Jesus; it is the differences and the divisions that have been reconciled through that relationship. So, it is not enough to share the faith with others just like you. That's a good start, but you've got to follow the Spirit's lead beyond the natural group.

Finally, the group will not be a church unless it is turning the world on its head. The purpose of the Catholic Church is not to end up with nice facilities, money in the bank, and a large congregation. No, the purpose of the Church is to redeem the world. The Church is not a retreat from the world or an enterprise that keeps its business separate from the world. The Church engages the world in order to change it.

These are some of the characteristics that must mark the Church you belong to. Whether your Church is the traditional parish or some other group that forms for the purpose of being a Church, these are the central standards by which to evaluate your Church's nature and mission. But it is essential to realize that if you follow Jesus, you will end up belonging to a Church and it is likely that the scent of mediocrity will linger in that Church. If you belong to the Catholic Church in the United States, mediocrity is guaranteed.

The biggest problem with the Church, if the truth be told, is all those other people who belong to the Church. If only we could get the teaching and the prayer, the good works and the rituals, the closeness to Jesus and the personal growth without all those other people getting involved. They just tend to screw it all up. Somehow, if we could attend a Church that was populated with actors and movie extras who followed their scripts perfectly - the priests and bishops, the choirs, the parish committees, the congregation all hired by a producer and coached by writers and directors – our experience of belonging to a Church would be so much more palatable and carefree. But, no, we have to deal with real people who, out of habit or choice, insist on belonging to the same Church we want to belong to and end up spoiling it.

It's sort of like the experience of going to the beach in the summertime. Going to the shore for swimming and sunbathing is one of the great pleasures for most residents of my home state, Rhode Island. Every weekend, individuals and families pack up the gear, the lotion, the towels, the blankets, the snacks, and head south or east to one of the beautiful beaches. Almost immediately, the experience is compromised: traffic. Traffic in the hot sun followed by lines at the parking lot, and inconsiderate people tossing trash on the ground, throwing balls too close to you, kicking sand on you as they run by, hogging the best spots in the water. The first thing that most beachgoers do when they arrive is to stake out and claim a spot on the sand where they can be most distant from the other people. (The rubric and pattern of choosing a spot on the beach is often mirrored by how people enter and sit down in Church – staking out a spot where they will not be too encroached upon by others). Besides ogling attractive bathers, most beach activities are ruined by the presence of others rather than enhanced. But people go, wishing that they could have the beach all to themselves but accepting the fact that they will have to put up with other people. In the same way, people belong to a church wishing that religious experience could somehow be presented to them in a pure, untouched way, but they reluctantly accept the fact that the Church is an organization of humans that necessarily, if unfortunately, involves other people.

Human involvement in a Church is often the scapegoat for everything that is wrong or questionable or controversial in the life of the Church as if you could have it another way. Often, people point their finger at this human element by using the distinction between "man-made" and "God-made." "That has no meaning because it is a man-made teaching." "That rule or custom is suspect because God did not institute it – it is man-made." Regardless if the matter is one of doctrine or rule, creed or ritual, organizational practice or decision, many people act as if it is possible to find a pure teaching from God that has not been tainted by humans, or a pure directive by God that has not been sullied by human interference, or a pure presence of God that is not spoiled by the human element, or a pure group experience of God that is not compromised by human sin.

Well, here's a newsflash: there is no pure Word of God that we can hear on earth. There is no pure presence of God that we can experience in the present life. There is no pure divinity that we can somehow touch apart from humanity. To think otherwise is to ignore completely the reality and lesson of the Incarnation. To think otherwise is to ignore what the basic social sciences teach us about how human beings experience any intangible in life. The divine has bound Himself to the human. The human and the divine belong together. That is the astounding reality of Jesus, and it is the even more astounding reality of the Church.

So, if you want to experience Jesus and share divine life, you must do it with other people and that involves all the "human stuff" that makes up the rest of everyday life: language, custom, organization, laws, roles, and on and on. For anyone who has actually belonged to a Church, that is very disheartening. They know all too well how much the whole enterprise of the Church really does get messed up by ignorance, pride, foibles, ambition, power-seeking, jealousies, arrogance, and all the rest that comes with the human package. There are many people who stay away from Church because of "all the hypocrites that attend that church." Do they really expect to find a group of people without a hair out of place? Do they really think they will somehow find God without having to get entangled with others just like themselves? Good luck.

Wrestling with the imperfections of the Church is a necessary part of responding to God's invitation to share his life. Ever since they wrote "see how they love one another," the community of believers has been not just the means of spreading Jesus' message, but also the message itself. The shared life of grace, here and now, is what we invite people to. How the members of the Church confront and overcome the wrong in the Church not only determines the effectiveness of the Church's witness to its beliefs, it also measures how much the Church reflects the divine life it is called to share. God's Love is made tangible in the life of the Church so it matters very much that all members of the Church struggle with and resolve its imperfections, its problems, and its sin. The Church is not only the means of bringing salvation to the world; it is also the product. If the Church is preaching love, it makes that message real in the love shared by members of the Church. If the Church is preaching justice, it actualizes that in the relationships of believers within the Church. The life of the Church puts flesh on the very things we hope for. When this particular group of people, the Church, overcomes jealousies and hatreds, dishonesty and selfishness, the life of grace comes alive. What a shame if we gave up on that challenge and promise.

There are moments when we witness the promise and transforming power of the Church and from those occasions we receive the blessed assurance that God's saving grace lives within this mediocre and disappointing institution and the hopeful determination not to let that organization stand still and fail its mission. One such moment for me was the last Holy Saturday I celebrated as an active priest. After celebrating the Easter Vigil in my own parish, I went at ten o'clock at night to a church that has since been torn down. At the time, it was the church with the largest seating capacity in the whole state of Rhode Island, a church once filled with Irish immigrants and their descendants. Now, Spanish-speaking immigrants were beginning to come and I was there to celebrate the Easter Vigil with them.

If you are not Catholic, you should go to an Easter Vigil, celebrated after sundown on the night before Easter Sunday. The texts and the prayers, the rituals and the symbols are so rich. Part of the ceremony is the lighting of the New Fire and, from that fire, the lighting of a large candle that symbolizes the Risen Jesus. Later, the whole goal of the Lenten season is reached when the congregation renews their vows of baptism. It is very ancient and it is very powerful.

On that night, about thirty people came. It was chilly, even inside the large church, and the people moved in close around the small fire that had been lit in a little charcoal grill resting on a tabletop. As I recited the prayers, I could look around and see everyone's face lit up by the glow from the flames. I felt a closeness to them. I felt that the faces reflected in that light were the faces of my brothers and sisters and I could see that my vows of baptism that I would renew that night were not only a pledge to the God out there and to the universal Church but were also a pledge to these people whose faces I could see by the light of the New Fire, a promise that

I would be Christ for them and, in turn, they, as they renewed their vows, were promising to be Christ for me.

It was a sense of Church that was stark and very scary; I saw, for a moment, what being baptized into a Church might mean, what entering into the Death and Resurrection of Jesus as a community might entail, this pledge of a life of self-sacrifice for people with whom I had no blood or social bond. I'm not sure that this dedication to the others is a characteristic of our parish communities. I know that I have not even attempted such a life beyond my family and some small circles of people I have known through the years. It is the great baptismal challenge for us who would be religious and church-going people that the renewal of our vows might mean a real and concrete commitment of love to the others who are gathered around the fire. Even more, it means going out and inviting more people to come closer to the New Fire.

Holding fast to these elemental experiences and to the great if anguished promise of the Church, what kind of Catholic Church can be formed in the United States to fulfill the mission that is entrusted to it in our time?

CHAPTER NINE

FORMING THE CHURCH OF THE FUTURE

M y friend, Mike, had taken up running marathons when he was a chaplain at Bowling Green University in Ohio. Not having been in contact in awhile, I asked him in a letter (before email or cell phones or texting), "Are you still running?" The answer came some time later via air mail letter, "Running?! No, I would be chased by lions." "Oh yeah," I thought. "That's right. He's in a different place now." Mike sure was. Born and raised in Toledo, Ohio, Mike had volunteered to go to the missions in Zimbabwe after several years of serving in a parish and then at Bowling Green as a priest of the Diocese of Toledo.

His years in Zimbabwe were life altering. Anyone who has traveled or lived away from familiar surroundings has more than likely returned home changed. Distance gives perspective. Differences give way to critique. The shedding of everyday environments and persona allow self-examination for those who dare, and exposes the essential and vital for the self-aware. Mike had had these sorts of experiences before, when he went overseas to study theology in Belgium. He plunged into it again when he stepped toward Zimbabwe. A different language. A different climate. A different culture. A different diet. Different architecture. Different clothing.

And a different Church. Mike was still a Catholic priest and it was still the Catholic Church but a very different Catholic Church. I asked Mike to write to me about his experience of the Church in Zimbabwe and, oddly enough, like me, a Holy Week memory came to his mind, only his memory was about a Holy Thursday celebrated with residents of a small village. Let me just relay his words:

> One of my most powerful experiences as a priest in Zimbabwe occurred during the celebration of Holy Thursday among a small Tonga village community. With no running water available, members of the community carried water in buckets on their heads from streams some 1-2 miles away. Needless to say, the river water was already somewhat dark and cloudy. Nonetheless, this was the water available to us for use during the Holy Thursday service. After reading the gospel passage about Jesus' service, one by one each Tonga child, youth and adult would reverently step forward to have their feet washed. There was no need to remove shoes as no one had shoes to wear. As we washed one another's feet, I was deeply touched as I felt with my hands their thick and calloused feet, roughened with deep crevices and cracks from years of walking barefoot. No one seemed to mind the darkness of the water as we cleansed their feet, dirty from walking on the ground. As each person's feet were being washed, the remainder of the community sang, danced in joyful rhythm and clapped their hands in support. This was an experience of the gospel at its core and

it shaped our small Tonga faith community into a Catholic community.

Following the washing of the BaTonga's feet, we experienced a period of gospel sharing and each person was given the opportunity to share how Jesus' washing of the disciples' feet touched their lives. During this sharing, the villagers discussed the needs of families suffering hunger from the drought, villagers distraught from elephants damaging their huts and fields, and concern for family members and friends dying of AIDS. Following the reflections, leaders were appointed to organize community service projects including "work for food" development projects, the formation of small groups to visit and pray with the sick and dying, and ideas as to how to approach the local government for help with the elephants. Service and social justice endeavors were formed, endeavors shaped by the gospel of Jesus.

Several small BaTonga faith-sharing groups met frequently for a couple years to share and reflect on the gospel and its impact on their lives. These periods of spiritual growth and dialogue allowed the light of Jesus' gospel to penetrate their culture, traditions and rituals – a deep sense of hospitality, their humor, their love of rhythm and dance, traditional healing herbs, their commitment to their ancestors, strong family ties; as well as their concerns with sickness, AIDS, divorce, adultery, witchcraft and alcoholism. Due to their interest in becoming servants of the gospel of Jesus in their culture, they chose to enter the Catholic Church. In a spirit of

      respect and mutuality, we witnessed the absorption
      of Jesus' gospel among the BaTonga in the birth and
      formation of new Catholic communities.

This was not the Church of Toledo where Mike grew up nor the Church of Providence where I grew up. This example of back-to-basics prayer and "parish" life – to which we will later return - in the BaTonga village stands in stark contrast to the highly organized and formal Catholic parishes known to most in the United States. But, they are all Catholic parishes and the same Church. Lived experiences of the Catholic Church can be very different from one another but still be of the Catholic Church. The essence of the Church – what gives it its identity as the Catholic Church – is mysterious but it is known by the believer, distilled from experience by the virtue of faith and marked as such through the infallibility of faith. If the Catholic Church can be the Catholic Church in different locales and in vastly different expressions in one person's lifetime (in this case, Mike's), it can remain Catholic over the course of time. The Catholic Church can survive transplantation across places; it can also survive evolution over time.

This is written by way of reassurance because the Catholic Church in the United States will undergo tremendous change over the next few decades. Whether by evolution or revolution, the Catholic Church will be vastly different in the not-so-distant future but recognizable, much like the resurrected Jesus, who was not immediately known by his friends but whose identity was indeed recognized, having survived the transformation of the resurrection.

This transformation will not be pretty. Change is difficult for most people and usually avoided or resisted. The Catholic Church has been changing in fundamental ways since the early 1940's when Pope Pius XII gave a green light to modern methods of studying Scripture, at the same time encouraging the faithful to read the Scriptures. Even though he did that in 1943 in his encyclical, *Divino Afflante Spiritu*, the good nuns and parish priests were still warning us in the early 1960's not to read the Scriptures without having a priest in the room (an exaggeration, of course, but the admonition against "going off on our own" when interpreting the Bible was unmistaken). The changes begun under the radar by Pius XII erupted into view and accelerated with the Second Vatican Council and the tumultuous years of the sixties and early seventies. The renovation of the Church wrought by Vatican II had its pluses and minuses but, overall, gave new life to a Church that was ill-positioned for its mission in the modern world.

There has been pushback on the changes mandated by the Second Vatican Council since they were set in motion. Even fifty years after the Council, a new translation of the prayers of the Mass in the United States was promulgated that amounted to a reactionary coup. While not a major issue compared to others, the movement to impose this translation represented hard line nostalgia and a desperate desire to reverse the clock, undo decades of change, and mount the Catholic religious experience as one would butterflies, beautiful but encased and lifeless. Change will, of course, continue outside of and within the Church, and this is a serious quandary for the Church even more so than for other institutions. The Church, after all, is charged with passing on a tradition and message that is not of its own making; its principal responsibility is to be a faithful steward of the saving message and mission that was entrusted to it by Jesus himself and so for twenty centuries the Catholic Church has had to balance faithfulness with adaptability: the need to be true to the Gospel while, at the same time, preaching and living it with sensibility and effectiveness in varying times and circumstances. Most certainly, the motivation of the "reactionaries" I criticize for resisting change is to preserve the truth of what has been handed on to us and to maintain the Church as a sure means of grace. For that they are to be admired. But they lack courage and the awareness that part of being "faithful" is relying on God to remain true to us through the risk and uncertainty required to engage a world that cannot understand the Gospel or respond to God's invitation unless it is spoken in words that are ever fresh and new. "See, I am making all things new" is God's hopeful but frightening declaration in the Book of Revelation.

The function of "adaptability" that the Church must fulfill suggests that there is a certain chameleon-like quality to the Church; the Church, it is presumed, can present itself, the message entrusted to it, and the life of grace lived by it, in various ways. That the Church has different presentations was established authoritatively in the book, *Models of the Church* by Avery Dulles. Cardinal Dulles presented five models of the Church in the first edition of the book in 1974 (the Church as Institution, Mystical Union, Sacrament, Herald, and Servant) and later added a sixth (Church as Community of Disciples). Each model is a lens through which we can see the nature of the Church, that is, how and what the Church must be to answer its calling. The list of models must continue to grow if we are to discover the Catholic Church that will fulfill its mission in the future.

There are certain models of the Church we must avoid adopting. The Catholic Church in the United States could very easily become the "Museum Church." It happened in Europe a long time ago, although being a "Museum Church" wouldn't have to be all that grim. Think of the many "living museums" that are found in almost every region: places where different historic periods or peoples are recreated. There is a great example of this in Massachusetts, a "museum" called Old Sturbridge Village where New England village life has been reconstructed as it was from 1790 to 1840. There are working farms and shops ringing a village green; actors actually do the work of the 1830's New Englanders, and visitors can walk through and observe how life at that time is remembered and speak with the farmers and artisans and laborers who respond to visitors as if it were still 1820. The Catholic Church in the United States could be that and, I suppose, it wouldn't be so bad. The Church could maintain a working model of Catholic life: prayers, customs, good works, and visitors could come to observe and perhaps be inspired by admirable practices or virtues and, maybe, even bring something into their own lives that they observed in the Museum Church, much like some visitors to Old Sturbridge Village take up candle-making or herb-gardening after visiting the living museum. If becoming the "Museum Church" meant that the function of the Church was providing the admirable to society rather than the essential, then that cannot be the model of the future.

The Catholic Church in the United States could also become the "Emily Post Church." In this model, the main focus of the Church would be ensuring that people are nice to each other. Stated more grandly, it would fall to the Catholic Church to function like Confucianism, laying out prescriptions for human relationships that lead to more harmonious societies and personal success. Churches have served this function for centuries, re-stating conventional moral wisdom, codes of conduct that were part of the culture but that didn't necessarily have any religious origin or inspiration. This is not unusual. Even in the Letters of St. Paul, there are some summaries of codes of behavior inserted now and then that can also be found in the pagan writings of his day; they were accepted standards of behavior that he endorsed or absorbed into his preaching about what the good life would be like. This sort of ethical reinforcement is important and, indeed, crucial to the overall working of society and it is something that churches ought to offer. However, it is a function fulfilled by the churches without breaking a sweat; there is nothing heroic displayed in being the "Emily Post Church."

What models will fit the Catholic Church of the future in the United States? Whatever they are, they must go beyond the Church being decorative. Fulfilling some non-essential functions in American society like bolstering people's emotional lives or reinforcing good citizenship does not get to the Church's essential mission as we have described it. To a large extent, this marginalization of religion in America, written about in Chapter Four, has already taken place in terms of the role of the Catholic Church in the public arena of American life. The Catholic Church along with other major denominations is also fading in terms of the actual numbers of people participating in church life. More and more people in the United States consider themselves "unaffiliated" when it comes to church membership. To say that the United States at the beginning of the twenty-first century is a godless nation is overstated. It is less and less of a church-going country; that much is known. A survey conducted by the Pew Forum on Religion & Public Life in 2012 matched findings of the National Opinion Research Center at the University of Chicago that revealed a thirty percent growth in Americans who considered themselves religiously unaffiliated in the first decade of the millennium. Nearly one in five Americans do not identify with any church. Tellingly, a large majority of these unaffiliated were raised in religious and practicing families.

The long-term change in the numbers of those who identify themselves as Catholic seems to be holding steady between 1972 and 2012; there is only a slight drop in numbers. The numbers of those affiliating with Protestant denominations declined much more precipitously. One might conclude that former Catholics are not among the increasing number of people who do not express any religious affiliation. This inference would be a false reading of the data, however. Immigration replenishes the ranks of Catholics in the United States that would otherwise be shrinking like the major Protestant denominations.

Fewer contributors may cause financial problems; the Church will have a harder and harder time justifying and maintaining its assets and infrastructure. But diminishing numbers are not the real problem. The real problem is diminishing impact. Regardless of the numbers, if the Church is not redeeming society it is failing. However the Catholic Church evolves in the United States in the coming years, the strategic planning that might direct that change must take as its mission statement Jesus' charge to his disciples in Matthew 28: 16-20, "Go, therefore, and make disciples of all nations. Baptize them in the name of the Father, and of the Son, and of the Holy Spirit. Teach them to carry out everything I have commanded you. And know that I am with you always, until the end of the world." In Jesus' vision expressed in these words, the energy of the Church is focused outward to those who do not belong to the Church. The Church's desire is to draw people into the Trinity, that is, to share God's very life. The fruit of this life of grace is a Church that acts to fulfill Jesus' expectations. The Church is confident and courageous in carrying out this mission because Jesus abides with his followers. It is that simple and that staggering.

The first step, then, of forming the Church of the future is to look outside of the Church. There is a wide world out there in desperate need of redemption, very far away from what God intended it to be. It is not the Eden of Genesis. It is not the Holy City of Revelation. Chapter Four discussed what could be the greatest evil of our time, the vast inequality between rich and poor. Chapter Six looked at another fundamental issue, the dignity and value of human life. Whether and how the Church brings its witness to bear on these matters will go a long way in determining if the Church intends to bring its saving message to all nations. There are other examples of how our world needs the transformation offered by God and that can be used as gauges for measuring the Church's impact.

Is it too late to talk about creeping materialism? Maybe it became raging materialism a long time ago. There is in the *zeitgeist* in which we now live – that is, in the spirit of our time – an appetite for reducing human activity and human beings to quantity and commodity: how much can be produced and what economic value can be fixed on that person or effort. Social communities have become markets; leisure time is becoming scarcer and scarcer. Play? No, in this world everyone is a worker. Even children don't do a lot of playing; the value of knowledge is measured by whether or not it leads to marketable skills. Utility is the new cardinal virtue; the value of people is determined by how useful they are to others' enterprises; the value of human activity is assessed by how much it increases a standard of living. Is there no one who is preaching and living a message that runs counter to the materialism in which we are steeped?

With the world reduced to the material, is it any wonder that relational life has been cheapened? In the world of abortion on demand, the mother-child relationship is a war zone. Sexual relationships are either devoid of meaning or only function to the advantage of one person, a continuous exercise in conquest or vacuity. The meaning of marriage is evolving, to put it politely. It is fortunate that the debate on same-sex marriage has intensified, forcing everyone to ask, "What is marriage, anyway?" Once we have that figured out, maybe we can turn our attention to defining "family." Certainly, exploring the nature, significance, and quality of human relationships should be a primary task of a faith community that defines God as "love" and that strives for new communities based on a kinship found in Jesus. Will the Church give voice to and provide example of what human relationships might be, redeemed and restored to original goodness?

Peace was the first gift of the resurrected Christ to his followers. It is the object of one of the most favored prayers of Catholics, the Prayer of St. Francis. Yet, widespread and lasting peace remains elusive. Instead, we live in a hyper-violent world. On any given day, in any of the major online news outlets, there is news of some unimaginable act of brutality that one human being has visited upon another. Some of the stories are so horrific as to be unreadable. And that is without consulting news stories about acts of war that dot the globe, consuming whole societies in spiraling and unending conflicts. Can the Church be not just a messenger of peace but also a constructor of peace?

Truth? What is truth? Pilate's question to Jesus, born of cynicism or bewilderment, is rarely asked today. Many do not believe that truth exists. Skepticism is the attitude into which people are born. The tyranny of perspective - that is, the notion that since every person experiences reality from a particular point of view people are prevented from ever approaching objective truth - has made the search for truth naïve and silly. The age of relativism and marketing and political posturing preaches that truth is whatever you can get people to believe. Just as materialism has reduced human activity to what is useful, so has the hyper-tolerance of the present day allowed the value of words to be judged by their utility, that is, how much they advance someone's interests rather than how much they reveal the truth.

There is, then, a catalog of ills plaguing the United States that cry out for healing and redemption: materialism, damaged relational lives, violence, confusion about what is worthy of our trust. Added to the devaluation of human life and the gaping inequality of the haves and have-nots, these disorders beg for a Savior. There is a Savior, but he lives on this earth through those who claim to follow him. We are not at the point of asking, is there a community of his followers making headway against these evils, or, is the Church having an impact? The question we are asking instead is, is there a community of Jesus' followers willing to take on these evils?

If the Church in the United States is to be a church that fulfills its mission in the future, then it has to be an organization that confronts evil in order to conquer it. "Do not be conquered by evil," writes Paul in Romans 12, "but conquer evil with good." To be that kind of Church requires different ways of thinking about the Church and church membership from what is current today; new models must be tried on, new templates developed. St. Paul used images such as putting on armaments or putting on a new persona in order to live out the Christian life effectively. In a similar way, we have to try on new frameworks for assessing the life of the Church that stretches our understanding and practice beyond the present boundaries. In the next two chapters, I will suggest "Martyrdom" and "Pilgrimage" as two lenses through which to view the Church and how it goes about fulfilling its mission.

CHAPTER TEN

MARTYRDOM

St. Agnes was a young woman who lived in Rome in the fourth century, who was two things no one wants to be these days: a virgin and a martyr. Her story is a little grisly and may not be too uplifting at first hearing; it may even be a little puzzling, making you shake your head.

Agnes was a Christian and just twelve years old when she was killed by state executioners for being a Christian. She, like so many others before her, had angered the "powers that be" by clinging to a religion outside the control of the state and viewed as dangerous to society. Christians were distrusted, engaging in secret and odd rituals that aroused suspicion and disgust. They were clannish, treating each other with peculiar regard (more positively it was said, "see how they love one another") and sharing some bond that was not in the everyday catalog of relationships: they weren't necessarily blood-related, they may not have been from the same ethnic background or class, they oftentimes did not share an educational background or professional interest. They did share an allegiance to someone who had been put to death by the government in a backwater region of the Roman Empire.

Agnes was one of them and, furthermore, she had taken a more drastic stance than most by declaring herself a virgin consecrated to "the Lord." This notion of being a virgin for a religious purpose was not unheard of at that time. Women were known to remain virgins to dedicate themselves to service in temples. Agnes, however, was not working in a temple, had dedicated herself to a Jewish activist, soothsayer or whatever, and had thus taken herself out of circulation, angering several potential and influential suitors.

Out of spite or civic duty, these men saw to it that this misguided young woman from that troublesome sect would be punished. More than likely, they were hoping that in the face of torture and a painful and gruesome death, Agnes would quickly abandon those strange beliefs and those despicable Christians and do what every red-blooded Roman girl should do: become a wife and join the household of a man of means.

It didn't work out that way. Confronted with chains and flames and the sword, Agnes signed herself with the cross and opened her arms in prayer. To the shock and disbelief of the crowds who had assembled, she was brutally murdered. All she had to do was renounce Jesus and get on with her life. She did not and her life was snuffed out at the age of twelve.

What are we to make of this virgin and martyr? For centuries after her death in the capital city, Christian writers would recount those awful events and hold up Agnes as an example for other Christians. They wouldn't let her story be forgotten and drew one lesson after another for others who would say they followed the same Jesus.

She hasn't been written or talked about in a long time. Such heroism has become rare and such zeal is very disturbing and even distasteful to the modern believer. One remark, written by Saint Ambrose a few centuries after her death, may shed light on her mind and heart and help us understand her a little better. He wrote, describing the scene at her death, "The crowds marvel at her recklessness in throwing away her life untasted, as if she had already lived it to the full."

"The crowds marvel at her recklessness in throwing away her life untasted, as if she had already lived it to the full." This statement, for me, captures the spirit of a martyr and begins to pinpoint the very things most of us believers are trying to avoid.

It is a little jarring to write this next observation while reflecting on St. Agnes and martyrdom, but at first hearing of this story, I was reminded of the old Kris Kristofferson/Fred Foster song lyric made famous by Janis Joplin, "Freedom's just another word for nothing left to lose." I was tempted to equate this type of freedom with St. Agnes' recklessness. But that's way off the mark. This was another kind of freedom altogether. Having been touched by the eternal, St. Agnes' regard for this world and this life was completely transformed. Filled with faith, hope, and love, she came to re-assess her whole life: her circumstances, her options, her life plans, the values held by her family, the paths towards which her interests were leading her - all of it – in view of her life in Christ. And then having found the eternal in herself, she made a choice and in that choice knew complete freedom. A few centuries before, St. Paul had a similar experience: "But those things I used to consider gain I have now reappraised as loss in the light of Christ. I have come to rate all as loss in the light of the surpassing knowledge of my Lord Jesus Christ. I have accounted all else rubbish so that Christ may be my wealth" (Philippians 3: 7-8). This experience that Paul and Agnes shared was a result of an encounter with Jesus, not the historical Jesus because neither had met Jesus as he walked the earth. They had come to know the Risen Jesus, something that is even possible for us in the twenty-first century. Through this relationship with Jesus and his followers, Paul and Agnes had emptied themselves of previously known points of orientation, of their fears, of their goals, of their satisfactions, of their estimations of what was worth effort and investment. They were then filled with an unfathomable love, a joy that could not be broken, a clear-eyed insight into what is most valuable, an unrelenting determination, and a steel courage. They would live life in Christ and witness it to others without counting the cost.

Agnes had left the normal boundaries that circumscribe our lives, the conventional wisdom and values according to which our choices are made and the trajectory of our lives assessed. What she decided to do really did appear reckless by those standards. In fact, her act of faith and witness was intentional and deliberate and self-possessed. It was an act that signaled a life completely committed yet completely unencumbered. She had become a believer open to martyrdom.

Can we be a Church open to martyrdom? If the Church Institution and Church as Sacrament and Servant can be suitable models for the Church, might it be that the Church as Martyr is the model needed in these next years? The stakes are high enough to warrant a life-and-death appraisal of what is contingent on believers' response to the condition of the world as we find it. Extreme poverty and suffering are acceptable collateral in the global economic game; the fate and value of human life rest on caprice in our country; right and truth is determined by those with the most power; human relationships are mocked and exploited; horrifying violence is a daily refrain; divisions along race and class and gender and ideology widen and harden. This degree of destruction and evil demands an equally profound witness to goodness and grace. The proportionate response is martyr-quality faith.

Sadly, martyr faith does not typify the Catholic Church in the United States. That there are individuals and even groups of Catholics who would step into Agnes' place is likely and, in fact, takes place still. But the Church as a whole does not possess the self-assurance, sense of identity or depth of conviction needed to conquer the evil that confronts it. Unlike in former days, allegiance and adherence to a distinct set of values cannot be presumed. Undistracted dedication to the person of Jesus and his teaching is not a given. The likelihood that belief will be chosen over the dominant culture is not high. It is not evident that the martyr's depth of commitment to the faith is present in our churches. A very plain and public example of this inadequacy, referred to earlier in the book, took place on May 17, 2009.

Notre Dame University, maybe the best-known Catholic university in the country, invited President Barack Obama to speak at its 164th commencement on that day and to receive an honorary doctor of laws degree. On its face, there was nothing unusual about that. Fifty-four percent of U.S. Catholics voted for Barack Obama. Furthermore, Notre Dame had conferred honorary degrees on other presidents and other presidents had delivered speeches at the university. Many Catholics objected to Notre Dame honoring President Obama, however. He was, after all, a politician who was diametrically opposed to the most fundamental moral teaching of their Church. Knowing his stance on abortion should have caused Catholics to reject him outright in the 2008 election regardless of his views on any other issue. The abortion issue is that fundamental. It is not one issue alongside many others. It's not that "Well, he got 8 out of 10 issues right so we'll overlook that fact that he advocates abortion at any time and for any reason or no reason." Abortion is a "starting gate" issue; if you don't get that right, there's no use in going any further. And so it was not surprising that a stormy if brief debate raged when Notre Dame's invitation became known. Some rightfully pointed out that invitations to other presidents could also have been called into question on similar grounds.

Mind you, if the president had been invited to Notre Dame to debate the abortion issue, that would have been fine. That was not the case, though. He was invited to offer unchallenged remarks and to be honored by the bestowal of a degree. At the time, I thought that the faithful and the hierarchy of the Church would bring every pressure to bear on the president of Notre Dame and Notre Dame's Board of Trustees to rescind this invitation and to state very clearly that rather than be honored by Catholics, President Obama should be condemned by Catholics for his stance on abortion. I expected that every single Catholic bishop in the United States would have publicly stated his opposition to this invitation. I expected every Catholic association from the Knights of Columbus to the Third Order of St. Francis to protest this invitation. I expected Notre Dame to have had enough fortitude to say, "We think Barack Obama is wrong. We think his extreme views on abortion are morally repugnant. We think that what he advocates is so intolerable that we don't want him or any politician who promotes those views on our property unless it is to discuss these issues candidly. Until he changes his stance, we will not give him university honors, we will not give him a forum, we will not give any legitimacy or credibility to his views, we will not lend him one ounce of support."

Needless to say, none of that happened. Yes, a handful of bishops, some alumni, and a few prominent Catholics did speak against the invitation. But on a nice spring day in South Bend, the speech was given, the degree was conferred, the event was reported nationally, and the Catholic faith in the United States suffered another blow. Notre Dame's and American Catholics' inability to stand for the most basic good raised the question, does being a Catholic in America have any meaning at all? When the time came to give witness, there was no martyr faith visible. Instead, a dissipated and incoherent Catholic faith was on display. While only a single incident, what happened at Notre Dame illustrates the current lukewarm nature of American Catholic faith. In the days leading up to the commencement ceremony, competing values won out over being followers of Jesus and his way of life. Other values were chosen, other goods pursued rather than life in Christ. No person or institution gave her life for the faith.

Is it necessary that every single member of the Catholic Church in the United States be ready to give his or her life for the faith? No. Not everyone is called to be a martyr, but an openness to martyrdom must be a prominent component of the Catholic Church for it to be a church. Part of that consciousness of the possibility of martyrdom is a realization of how much the Catholic faith is distinct from the American culture and not running away from that fact. The American dream is not necessarily Jesus' dream. Assimilation into the political and cultural mainstream is not necessarily a worthy goal for American Catholics. If the presence of believers in the United States goes unnoticed then either we have reached the end time in which "the earth is filled with knowledge of the Lord as water covers the sea," (Isaiah 11) or Catholics have achieved a spiritual blandness that allows them to be undetectable as they go about their everyday lives. The latter seems to be the case. A Church that is not challenging the dominant culture is in no danger of being persecuted.

Has openness to martyrdom been replaced by a stronger desire for self-preservation? The American Catholic Church as an institution and American Catholics as individuals have a lot invested in the status quo. There is a nationwide network of dioceses and parishes, a sizeable healthcare network, a significant educational system, and charitable institutions embedded in local communities. There are political alliances and voting blocs, formed by ethnic and economic bonds more so than religious ties that span a few generations. Catholics have come to be a dominant presence in corporations and government. Largely the descendants of immigrants, Catholics have climbed socio-economic ladders to reach prominent and essential positions in American society, sharing a culture that appears to have become more formative than the creed professed at Baptism when it was proclaimed, "This is our faith. This is the faith of the Church. We are proud to profess it in Christ Jesus our Lord." Can this institution and these Catholics meet the measure of the martyrs' commitment and stake everything on openly following Jesus?

People and institutions risk it all for values and causes and persons they consider "core" and that touch every aspect of their lives or organizations. This deference to what is central down to the smallest matters is evident even in the most ordinary. Ask devoted parents if there is anything they do or any decision they make that is not, in some way, related to the well-being of their children. Ask elite athletes if there is anything about their lives that is not, in some way, referenced back to the sport in which they excel. Ask entrepreneurs if they only pay attention to their ventures part of the time. Not possible. In the same way, the faith of a martyr is the preeminent and all-consuming reality in his life. There is no element in his life that escapes its influence. Can this be said of our dioceses and parishes? What is it that occupies their attention and efforts? Are they marshalling all their resources - financial and human – to preach the message of Jesus? And what about the individual Catholics themselves? Are they anchoring their lives in Jesus? Are they redeeming the worlds they occupy? Or do they compartmentalize their lives in such a way that their faith does not touch how they approach their jobs, their loves, their pastimes, how they vote, how they invest, how they purchase, how they raise children? A Church that would have martyr-faith has a focus and devotion so complete that it is all-consuming, approaching a certain level of fanaticism. If the spreading of the Gospel is to be the dominant consideration, have American Catholics allowed this mission to infiltrate every aspect of their lives, to reach into every choice and action just as a martyr would? Bringing all resources and efforts to bear on preaching the message of Jesus is the first principle around which all churches have to prioritize and all Catholics have to evaluate how they are living. The truth of the matter is that in most dioceses and parishes there is no shared mission, no awareness that households and parishes have a common goal towards which they are contributing and for which they are responsible.

How different are Catholics willing to be in present-day America? Can Catholics profess a faith and still pretty much resemble their non-Catholic neighbors in terms of their life pursuits and orientation? If martyr-quality faith requires sacrifice perhaps not of one's life – the ultimate sacrifice – but of comfort and status and lifestyle and assets and peaceful co-existence, is there a willingness to place all those things and more at risk for the sake "of affecting and as it were upsetting, through the power of the Gospel, mankind's criteria of judgment, determining values, points of interest, lines of thought, sources of inspiration and models of life, which are in contrast with the Word of God and the plan of salvation?" (*On Evangelization in the Modern World*, Pope Paul VI)

These are the questions that confront U.S. Catholics and that challenge them to give witness to their faith. The witness that the Catholic Church in the United States is being called to give is not a witness born of hate or hostility or superiority, but of love and service. The Church need not declare war on the rest of American society, although there will be conflict. The Catholic Church need not draw battles lines, although it will encounter hostility. Sharing life in Christ in every sphere of life will inevitably lead to struggle because the message and values to which Catholics bear witness will clash with and challenge mainstream culture as well as powerful political and economic interests. If American Catholics wish to be a martyr Church, they will find themselves engaged in a struggle but it ought not be warfare fueled by animosity and hatred. For Catholics, the fight always has to be preceded by prayer and good works directed toward those who oppose what God intends for the world He created. It is a fight in which the standard for Christians must be Jesus' startling words "Love your enemies," and his basic insight that redeemed human relationships are not built on power but on love. Following the dictum of St. Paul in the twelfth chapter of the his letter to the Romans, "Do not be conquered by evil but conquer evil with good," Christians struggle for God's reign firm in their belief that while they will not overcome the world by use of power, neither will they give in to power.

Acting on the central issues confronting the Church that have been described in the preceding chapters will mean that American Catholics take on the heart of a martyr. No lower a level of commitment, no less consuming a focus, no smaller willingness to risk it all is called for. Believers and Church structures will have to expose their security, safety and comfort to violent change in order to claim and advance the mission of the Church. Accompanying this willingness to act recklessly is a sense of urgency that is characteristic of a martyr's faith, a need to draw a line in the sand, a resolve to take a stand here and now. The all-in commitment and all-consuming reach that characterizes a martyr's faith is enlivened by a sense that sacrifice cannot be put off, that an action must be taken, a statement must be made, or a confrontation must take place now. There is no feeling that maybe this is something that can wait or that he or she hasn't reached the point at which she has to give her life.

Action alone is always insufficient. Prayer is the start and the finish of any martyr's witness. In various times and places in the history of Church, even the simple and unobtrusive act of prayer leads to martyrdom; overt acts of faith, public confrontations with authority or hostile groups were not the sole prelude to giving one's life for the faith. In 1291, in the last years of the Crusades, about two hundred years after the first Crusade, there was a Carmelite monastery on Mount Carmel in the Carmel mountain range in what is now northwestern Israel. During the Crusades, Mount Carmel had often changed hands between the warring parties. One night, the monks were praying the final prayer of the night, Compline, and as they were singing the traditional hymn to the Blessed Mother, the *Salve Regina*, the Saracens forced their way into the monastery and slaughtered the monks as they sang. That seems like a long time ago and, as has been noted earlier in the book, martyrdom can seem very remote both in time and possibility. Jump ahead seven hundred years, then, to another monastery, this one in Tibhirine, Algeria. A small group of Trappist monks lived a simple life of prayer, manual labor and hospitality there, but in March 1996 the Armed Islamic Group kidnapped them and two months later they were executed. Sometimes, even a dedicated life of prayer openly lived can lead to persecution and martyrdom.

Martyrdom is not remote in time. Open Doors International reported in 2013, that 2,123 Christians were killed because of their faith, twice as many as in 2012. In many countries, then, martyrdom is very real, but it has become a remote possibility in the United

States. The outcome of the Church's central mission depends on American Catholics' willingness to bring martyrdom within their everyday horizon once again. If being a Martyr Church can operate as a model for Catholics in the United States, the experience of Pilgrimage can show American Catholics how to be such a Church in the years ahead.

CHAPTER ELEVEN

THE CHURCH OF THE FUTURE: PILGRIMAGE

I don't know if Mother Teresa looked any taller when she was younger and not stooped as we saw her in later years. Perhaps, but she was a tiny woman at any age. Lined and wrinkled was her face. Her most prominent physical feature? Her eyes. Dark. Infinite. Filled with pathos, a blend of sadness and compassion. Many have mentioned the peace and, even, joy that exuded from her and while I am sure that their sensibility is on the mark I would offer another reading of Mother Teresa, and I know this is not a pleasant comparison. I would say that Mother Teresa closely resembled a Holocaust survivor, exhibiting in her body the same sort of exhaustion, deprivation, suffering, and witness of unimaginable evil.

Following the release of the book *Mother Teresa: Come Be My Light: The Private Writings of the Saint of Calcutta* by Rev. Brian Kolodiejchuk, there was considerable discussion of the meaning of Mother Teresa's admission of the loss of her awareness of the divine presence. In the years 1946-1947, just before her call to work with the poor of Calcutta, she experienced a deep mystical union with God in her prayer. After that, though, once she started her independent service of the destitute in the streets, God disappeared – for almost fifty years Mother Teresa had no sense that God was there when she prayed. She wrote to a confessor, "There is no God in me."

Her "fans" are more than a little thrown off. Most of us like to think that praying is as easy and satisfying for saints as shooting a few hoops might be for pro basketball players. Apparently, that wasn't the case. Her detractors (yes, Mother Teresa has detractors!) are only too happy to have this evidence of the silliness of her belief in God and the band-aid nature of her work for the poor. It really is sacrilegious of these critics to tear her down. It is possible to find fault with Mother Teresa and her approach to poverty and the religious life. However, that the world was dealing with a person who had a profound contact with God there should be no doubt. Her willingness daily to confront suffering and evil with charity for so many years is testimony to many intangible realities that escape the modern soul.

Mother Teresa's difficult spiritual fate was a result of two things: her desire to unite herself with Jesus on the cross and her goal of worshipping him in the distressing disguise of the poor. Her identification with Jesus ensured that she would experience the anguish and abandonment he felt on the cross, the barometers measuring the intensity of evil, telescoped from over the centuries, that confronted His love. Her identification with the poor would bring her face to face with that same suffering and evil.

Jesus' act of self-sacrificing love that is at the heart of the Christian experience was characterized by St. Paul in his Letter to the Philippians as "kenosis," a Greek word that means "emptying," a pouring out of oneself on others' behalf without counting the cost. Having done this in her own life, Mother Teresa was indeed left with an unfathomable emptiness.

One can return to the Holocaust to glimpse a similar emptiness, a similar absence of the divine. In his foundational book *Night*, Elie

Wiesel recounts his experiences as a twelve and thirteen-year-old in Auschwitz and nearby concentration camps from 1944 until the end of the war in 1945. World War II and the complete collapse of civilization is one bookend of modern times. It inaugurated the era in which we live that has been marked by evil and the elusiveness of God. Eliezer Wiesel was twelve going on thirteen and a very faith-filled and spiritually advanced youngster when he and his family were sent to the camps. Wiesel writes, "Never shall I forget that night, the first night in camp, that turned my life into one long night seven times sealed. Never shall I forget that smoke. Never shall I forget the small faces of the children whose bodies I saw transformed into smoke under a silent sky. Never shall I forget those flames that consumed my faith forever. Never shall I forget that nocturnal silence that deprived me for all eternity of the desire to live. Never shall I forget those moments that murdered my God and my soul and turned my dreams to ashes. Never shall I forget those things, even were I condemned to live as long as God Himself. Never."

Notice the silence and absence of God that he mentions, echoed in later years by Mother Teresa. For Elie Wiesel (who, by the way, remained a man of faith albeit a qualitatively different faith), the actions of the Nazi's in the camps were not the only evil; in the minds of many prisoners was the complicity of the rest of German society and, indeed, the rest of the world. I believe that in her encounters with the poorest of the poor in Calcutta and throughout the world, Mother Teresa came face to face with that same evil. How can it be that millions live and die in the misery of the concentration camps of slums while the world is indifferent? She was courageous enough to embrace that darkness and to enter the world where God's consolations disappeared. Mother Teresa's faith stepped into another dimension as she held to the belief that beyond the heart of darkness lies the light of the Creator.

Mother Teresa's bleak faith is iconic of the spiritual life of humanity following the Second World War even until today. God is not readily evident; humanity does little to reveal Him. Those who would believe do not find it easy. In such a circumstance, when God has been so distant as to be imperceptible, it has been the impulse of believers – and those who want to be believers – over the centuries, to seek out the divine, even as God is seeking them. To find God, to experience his presence, people have gone on pilgrimage. Pilgrimage has been a task for believers in all centuries and many faiths. Believers, or those who want to be, go to what they regard as a blessed place, perhaps made that way by a special personage or event. They look for grace, an experience of God's presence, and they leave their ordinary lives to make a journey, oftentimes joined by others, to a destination at which they hope to be touched by the divine. Maybe they want their faith renewed; maybe they want a portion of faith itself. They may go to be healed; they may go to be broken from ways of life that have become burdensome. Perhaps they seek forgiveness, or the power to forgive someone else. Some go to keep a promise; some go to make one. Maybe they go to say, "thank you," maybe they go to beg. Compelled or drawn, they journey.

The experience of pilgrimage is wonderfully captured in a beautiful book a friend of mine wrote *Field of Stars*, about one of the pilgrimages he made to Campostela, Spain, which is one of the most famous pilgrim routes and destinations in Europe. The apostle James is supposed to have gone to Spain and preached and died there. Pilgrims have gone to his tomb for centuries. My friend Kevin walked over five hundred miles to reach Campostela and he chronicles his outer and inner journey over the course of those thirty-five days. In doing so, he describes some experiences of the pilgrim that, in my view, demonstrate why pilgrimage might be recommended as a paradigm for how to be a Catholic Church in the United States.

What is most fundamental to being a pilgrim is that he or she is on the move. It is not aimless movement since there is a destination and there are inspirations that act as guides and anchors for the pilgrim's journey, but it is movement nonetheless. This mobility that is essential to being a pilgrim is so suitable to the culture in which we live. So much of what we do used to depend on our being in one place: work, communication, entertainment, knowledge seeking and sharing. That is no longer the case. With each new device, people's worlds are moving with them. This is the experience of the pilgrim. It is not only mobility that makes the pilgrim's world so much like the world of the twenty-first century. What is equally striking is the how the pilgrim's experience of community resembles what we are seeing in the present age. Take as an example a very riveting video that can be accessed online of a "flash mob" of singers and musicians who assembled in the courtyard of the Boston Museum of Art around Christmastime to perform "O Holy Night." Besides the beauty of the performance itself, the faces and reactions of the people who just happened to be there reveal how meaningful this event was for them. Having such beautiful music and sentiments drop unexpectedly into one's day was akin to the Incarnation itself by which God entered the ordinary. For several minutes, musicians and singers formed a group that was conscious of being a group, and the audience itself also had a communal experience that cast everyone in the room as belonging to a distinct and privileged group. And then this "community" disappeared. Flash mobs have this effect whether their focus be profound or silly.

Besides "flash mobs," the digital world has produced smart mobs and "friends" and "followers" and "subscribers" and groups of people gathered around fandoms, blogs, Tumblr and Instagram accounts and all manner of what makes up social media. It is not a stretch at all to say that in the digital world, a whole new way of experiencing community has arisen. Sure, these are not families or deep friendships or communes, but they are meaningful connections that are made among disparate people. The depth and quality of such digital relationships can rival what is found in many parish communities.

On a pilgrimage, the pilgrims form communities almost randomly. Two, three, or four people find themselves walking together and begin conversations and games and songs and prayer.

They stop at "refugios," small hostels or inns that cater to the pilgrims passing along the way. Small groups gather to eat together, to share stories from the road, to tend to each other's wounds and aches and pains. But these small communities of pilgrims quickly dissipate and change and new groups are formed as the walk continues with new challenges to face together and new things to share. There is very little that is permanent; the only thing that remains constant is the journey and the destination. As these small communities form and disappear, take shape and then change, they are all conscious of being part of a larger community, a bigger movement of pilgrims who are being pushed and led by the same Spirit. There are few requirements to be a member of the pilgrim community. The standards are minimal, but there are standards. Are you willing to walk the walk? Are you willing to maintain this focus on the journey? Although the many communities that are formed along the way do not last, what is shared among the pilgrims is no less profound because of its fragile and temporary nature. It is real and meaningful and its effects can be lasting. Saying that pilgrim communities are "changing" has two meanings. One is, as we have seen, that the size and make-up of these communities change. They are pliable and porous. The other way the communities change is that they are undergoing conversion. As they walk and live through the pilgrimage, they are becoming different people and they undergo the transformation that comes from grace.

A pilgrimage is a curious blend of community and individual effort. Walking for hours on end in silence, lost to one's own thoughts, testing one's limits physically, mentally and spiritually, and confronting whatever inner baggage one has been carrying, sometimes for a lifetime, is a very solitary exercise. At the same time, as one encounters other pilgrims, with people catching up to one another, joining one another as people stop to rest, assembling at *refugios*, and tending to each other's needs, there is a growing sense that this very individual undertaking is one that is shared. An awareness overtakes each person that he or she is one among a long line of pilgrims stretched out over hundreds of miles, all enveloped in a single purpose, engaged in a common contest. The journey seems self-directed but as pilgrims progress along the ancient route, they become aware that they are being led and that this is no longer *my* journey or *my* project but a public undertaking shouldered by a community.

This odd combination of solitude and community is matched by an equally peculiar mix of structure and disorder. The route is set and there is an established system of *refugios* and people who staff them (*hospitaleros*). The way is fairly well marked so that pilgrims will not get lost. Progress is documented by stamps or seals to verify that, in fact, the pilgrim has put in the miles. Within this structure, however, considerable unpredictability and novelty exist. Moods and motivations shift. Interior discoveries surprise or even frighten the pilgrims. Plans about how far to walk on a given day change. A variety of people assume or are given authority depending on the need or challenge facing the groups traveling together, and the groups themselves, as has been noted, are constantly expanding, shrinking, and changing their members. The extent to which pilgrims' activity is structured or formalized is determined by the mission: how banding together and organizing help to reach the destination.

The destination really determines it all. Time, resources and effort are all concentrated on accomplishing the pilgrims' goal, doing whatever it takes to complete the journey but doing nothing additional. The pilgrims' life is reduced to essentials: no extra baggage, no unnecessary assets. The pilgrims' state is transitory. Nothing is permanent about pilgrimage except the interior conversion that takes place and the growth in grace.

Being a Church on pilgrimage may suit Catholics in the years ahead more than the parish and diocesan structures we have now. Gatherings initiated by believers may become more commonplace. Rather than waiting for the schedule of services or parish activities, congregants might convene prayer or action on their own. Communities of believers might form around a cause or event instead of a central location, brought together by a shared interest or attraction. They may endure or they may disappear; membership will have a great deal of elasticity and much may be ad hoc or temporary. A pilgrim Church would have a very local flavor with small groups of people coalescing around a specific focus, but these pilgrim Catholics would also identify with a larger movement. Parishes and dioceses would not vanish or become irrelevant but the spiritual and organizational dynamics would change. The same sorts of de-centralization and increased flexibility that governments, corporations, and many enterprises are experiencing will affect the Church as well.

You must see, then, that the heart of the pilgrim closely resembles the heart of the martyr: the intense focus, the "all in" commitment, the abandonment of permanence, the thirst for a moment of grace that changes their life orientation, the radically different assessment of what is worth the investment of time and strength, the embrace of suffering and sacrifice in order to reach a goal, the acceptance of considerable uncertainty, knowing the destination but not knowing what will happen on the way. A Church with this heart is the Catholic Church needed in the United States. The experience of both the pilgrim and the martyr can inform the Catholic Church in the twenty-first century. The Church as Martyr and the Church as Pilgrim stand as two ways for the Church to be in the years that are rushing towards us.

The Church that might be the Pilgrim Church and the Martyr Church in the future must know that there is a great deal at stake, enough to set out on a journey leading away from the ordinary paths of life, enough for which to give one's life. The disordered condition in which the United States finds itself with materialism that dominates our culture, a landscape of relational life that has become a wasteland, destructive violence, crippling skepticism, blindness to the value of human life, and a scandalous gulf between rich and poor cannot be healed and redeemed unless there is a community of believers willing to invest the goodness and virtue that is needed to bring about what God intends.

Being that kind of a Church means, first of all, recognizing that Catholics are different from the rest of American society, that we are on a different journey just as pilgrims are, that we have different goals, different values, and a different life-orientation as martyrs have. This awareness must be coupled with a deep commitment to Jesus and to others who follow him. It requires a willingness to risk it all, to shed whatever we would cling to that might make us hesitate in answering Jesus' call to respond to the needs we see. Being that kind of Church asks that we leave nothing in our lives beyond the reach of the redemptive power of grace. Most of all, it means that sharing Jesus' life with others becomes our highest priority, the focus of our family and relationships, at our work and in our schools, and in the political and economic spheres in which we live. The constant stance of such a Church is invitation, a desire openly expressed through word and action that our society experience the fullness of life envisioned by God at the beginning of Creation.

Becoming that Church may mean that the Catholic Church in the United States embrace a new understanding of authority, moving away from the need to keep order and, instead, making a act of faith that God will remain with us as we engage the world through actions that lend credence to clear and strong preaching of the Gospel. It may mean a letting go of assets and goals that have consumed much of our attention. It may mean broader admittance to ministry. It may mean a re-deployment of resources: the schools, hospitals, universities, and parishes that are the backbone of the institutional Church. It certainly means a laity that asserts its faith in boardrooms, legislative chambers, marketplaces, media, and higher education.

Above all, the Church that walks the uncertain path of the pilgrim and embraces the risks of the martyr will need to be courageous. Courage is a virtue that is based both on a sober assessment of reality and a decision to be reckless, to act without counting the cost even when the cost is known. A timid Church will not be able to meet the challenges that face us in the twenty-first century.

It is not enough for individuals to come forward to be pilgrims and martyrs. That will be insufficient and it will not last. Jesus is alive through a community. Jesus is fully alive in the sharing of everyone's gifts in the Church. We will need each other to be successful in the mission entrusted to us. It is a great comfort and strength to know that a saint such as Mother Teresa accompanies us in this project. She has been a saint for the modern times. She sought the God who had disappeared. She left behind a comfortable structure to try something new. She met evil with charity. She emptied herself for others, sharing in the self-sacrifice of Jesus. One of her best-known sayings is that holiness is not the luxury of the few but the simple duty for us all. Her courageous faith shows what is possible for all of us.

EPILOGUE

It has been many years since I began to jot down notes and write longer texts that eventually became what you find in this book. For the longest time I wanted to describe what ails the Church and then write a prescription for how to heal and reform the Church. Besides discovering how presumptuous such a goal is, I have since learned that the nature and health of the Catholic Church is, first of all, the work of the Holy Spirit, and, secondly, the product of people and forces that can barely be enumerated or understood – which is why I began this book on a personal note and end on one. Close to eighty million Americans count themselves as Catholic. I am one of them. You the reader are one among millions. How each of us conducts himself or herself in the face of the many challenges I outlined in this book doesn't seem to count for much. But it's all each of has to give.

From my days in St. Edward School, I still believe that our individual efforts have eternal significance. As many have observed, our contribution to the greater good is only one drop in the ocean, but it is the drop that would not be there unless we offer it. And so I am offering these words to other Catholics and other people of good will fully aware of their limited value but fully hopeful that they can be one addend in the greater sum of believers' contributions to fulfilling the mission of the Church. Regardless of how we analyze the life of the Church or map out possible courses of action, nothing will come of it unless we make a connection between our personal lives and the universal mission Jesus entrusted to his followers so many years ago. Recognizing that intersection and acting upon what it suggests is crucial to the Church's fulfilling its promise. Surprisingly, how much each of us invests in this mission will influence its outcome. It is a sobering truth that the possibility of redeemed families and redeemed communities and a redeemed nation depends on our responses to Jesus' call.

That Jesus is asking something of each of us there is no doubt. The central task of our time on earth is to discern what that might be and to do whatever we can to accomplish those things Jesus calls us to do. Much can get in the way. Sometimes we are so busy about something else, we are deaf to Jesus' call. Sometimes we are paralyzed by feelings of inadequacy or powerlessness. Sometimes we are daunted by the immensity of the task or the amount of effort needed. However, Jesus does not ask us to make the pilgrimage in a day. He just wants us to start.

Start by being a church. Wherever you are and whoever you are with, be a church. Don't wait to get permission; don't start a building campaign; don't start a membership drive; don't draw up by-laws; don't outline an organizational chart. Keep it simple. Keep it basic. Think of the BaTonga people my friend Mike prayed with and ministered to and how they went about forming a church. Think of the elements of a church described earlier in the book.

First of all, find at least one other person with whom to share this journey. A spouse? A son or daughter? A co-worker? A friend or neighbor? If it is one person, a few, or many, gather together as a group brought together by Jesus. Regardless of the relationships that may already exist in the group, it will be the shared relationship with Jesus that will make you a church. Gather together and pray. Maybe praying together is all you will do at first. It doesn't matter because this will be the most important thing that you ever do.

Then, be Christ for one another. Take seriously your vows of baptism and make them a public declaration that you are sons and daughters of God, brothers and sisters in Christ, filled with the same Spirit, sharing joyfully in the life of grace. This service of one another will begin to turn outward. Just as the BaTonga imagined very concretely what washing each other's feet meant, your church will look to serve the rest of the world, especially the poor and especially sinners.

As the church matures, it will follow the Spirit's lead beyond itself to ever-expanding relationships. Who will be invited into this church? What boundaries and differences will this shared relationship with Jesus overcome? It will not be enough to share the faith with others similar to you. The Spirit of Love will form communities beyond ordinary bonds.

Finally, the group will find itself engaging the world so that it can be redeemed. This is when the martyr and pilgrim qualities of the church will be most pronounced as your church, no matter the size or makeup, begins to live and witness to its graced life openly. It is at this point that we will need a certain amount of courage as this book implies.

How our churches with a small "c" might align with the bigger Church of our parishes, if we are active in one, or of our dioceses is an unknown and not a major concern as we go about the business of being a church. Questions about authenticity and authority that wonder if what people are doing in these small churches is "Catholic" will inevitably arise, and they will have to be answered, but that should not deter anyone from stepping out and acting as a believer and a Catholic. The world is changing, and how large organizations such as governments, corporations, and churches operate is changing as well. De-centralization is a hallmark of this change, and that means that small, unorganized initiatives that grow are the rule of the day, and this shift will be a factor in shaping the Church of the future.

Now that this book is shared, my family and I are reassessing our religious lives just as I am expecting that others might do. That is an exciting and happy prospect. The disquiet anyone might feel about the Catholic Church can lead to cynicism and despair, or a renewed search for God's will and a desire to live the life of grace with others in a new way. I hope that your reading this book encourages you to do the latter and to bear witness to the One who is making all things new.